The
Profit
Hunters

Tales of mischief
in the countryside

Bill Doherty

"Romany"

Published by Skycat Publications 2013
Vaiseys Farm, Cock Lane, Brent Eleigh, Sudbury, Suffolk CO10 9PA
Tel 44 (0) 1787 248476
info@skycatpublications.com

Printed in England by Healeys Printers
17 Farthing Rd, Ipswich, Suffolk IP1 5AP, United Kingdom
Tel 01473 461122
www.healeys-printers.co.uk

ISBN 978 0 9575673 1 3

© Bill Doherty 2013

Contents

About the Author

BILL WAS BORN in the mining town of Bedlington in Northumberland in 1955. From an early age his interest in wildlife and the countryside was evident, being involved in almost every form of countryside pursuit, over a time span of almost 50 years.

Bill began keeping and breeding British finches with his father John, and at 15 years old he was a founder member and committee member of the newly formed Blyth and Bedlington Cage Bird Society. The pair were noted exhibitors of cage birds in Northumberland for many decades. Bill's speciality was producing hybrids, crosses between various British finches, breeding these in cages, rather than the larger flights used by other breeders.

Bill left school at 15 and served an apprenticeship as a motor mechanic and stayed in the motor industry for 35 years.

With his father, Bill kept, worked and bred both lurchers and Scottish deerhounds, forming the Kennel Club affix of Doxhope Deerhounds, the kennel was noted for producing sound working stock, until the death of John in the early nineties. Both Bill and John judged many lurcher shows in England and Scotland.

Other countryside activities that Bill participated in included being a mole man, glass engraver, taxidermist, stick dresser, angler, fence erector, vermin controller, ringer with the BTO, conservationist, writer and countryside diarist.

As a writer Bill achieved qualifications in creative writing, and has had over 100 articles published in the UK sporting press, in magazines including the Countryman's Weekly, Cage and Aviary Birds and the Birdkeeper.

The Profit Hunters is the third book written by the author, the first two being *A Bird in the Hand* and *Working Deerhounds, Lurchers and Longdogs,* both published by Skycat Publications.

Bill now works in health and social care, and has graduated and lectures and trains at various colleges in Northumberland, he also trains in various areas of health and social care for the employment services, private companies and is a trainer for Newcastle city council adult services.

Wildlife photography is now the main interest of Bill the profit hunter, exhibiting and presenting on the subject, and also winning various prodigious competitions.

Introduction

TREADING somewhat less energetically down that narrow road named "growing old", I realize just how much information has been retained during my exploration of life's shadows. Memories of exciting jaunts and secret exhilarating adventures into Mother Nature's back gardens lie thick and heavy on the boughs of time, and it is my belief that many of these experiences may nourish the appetite of countless folk who may be curious or interested in the ways of the countryside, so it is partly due to this premise that once again I have been spurred to put pen to paper.

The era in which my aging body has been so privileged to exist could be deemed as fairly modern times, however my soul remains confined to an era where push and rush are forbidden, and my mind remains ambling along quiet country lanes revealing a cornucopia of interesting finds. It was during this bygone era that many individuals taught me many secrets of the countryside. Time has allowed me the great fortune of witnessing countless happenings, plus many changes that have affected our countryside and the wildlife it houses, some for the better, some however for the worse. God has blessed me with a photographic memory that has ensured all that has been seen is remembered as if documented in a manuscript, and from whose pages I can rewrite for others to enjoy.

In its conception this "book for the country person" was primarily a manuscript of entertainment, partly through written documentation of hunting possibilities while emphasizing what myself, and men of similar thinking have achieved, individuals highly skilled in such diverse, and in most cases, unlawful countryside pursuits. It was

also my prerequisite to furnish readers with some finer details of the surreptitious breed of countryside characters and likable rogues that my existence has had the privilege of knowing, some whose night time vigils begun as the day for others peacefully ends. A brand of men who because of their experience and understanding of the countryside had so much to offer, but, unfortunately who are becoming more and more uncommon in today's lazy, wanting for nothing society.

Where illicit hunting is concerned, for me there has always existed a recognised hierarchy with regards to men-o-the-fields. On the bottom rung of the hunting ladder there is the part-time poacher come occasional hunter-gatherer, a person well and truly worth his weight in pigeon shit. A lacking of courage and drive ensured a person from this group may constantly have talked the talk, but this is an individual who ventured out on jaunts akin to a nervous rabbit never far from safety for fear he had to make a quick get away from a dangerous shadow or ruthless noise.

According to self praise, that poor recommendation, these fellows possess such unbelievable ability when out in the fields, quite amazing considering how they favour relaxing happily in their warm homes, dreamily gazing into Mick Cawston prints that adorn each spare gap on every wall, or browsing in amazement at the latest kill crazy lurcher book, while outside in a theatre that is the countryside where first-class accomplishments and great poaching reputations are made, an angry wind wails like a Banshee through the tired, leafless branches of fiercely swaying trees, and the heavens, devoid of stars are as black as ink.

Dressed akin to a country squire in every fashion-friendly brand name imaginable and smelling of Pacho-Rabane after-shave, terror and apprehension cloud this fellow's mind, scared, for fear his hair blows out of place or mud pays an unwelcome visit to his new green Wellingtons or god forbid, behind his well manicured fingernails. Any knowledge he possesses arrives via the pages of poorly written books or articles in sporting magazines begat by novice hunters, and the greater element of experience on his hunting CV has been stolen from conversations with others, who may know a bit. God only knows when time is found to venture out in pursuit of bird or beast with such an abundance of exciting events going on in the life of this meagre countryman.

Sitting comfortably on the next rung and a little further up in the pecking order there were those more successful takers of game, men that may have actually achieved some successful hunting days and good killing nights, albeit in a part-time capacity. They may indeed have furtively travelled finch-infested hedgerows with bird trappers, or now and again run the gauntlet of crafty well organised bailiffs on singing burns and roaring rivers, but throughout their proletarian endeavours unfortunately they learnt virtually nothing from these incidents, and, the result was someone well and truly bitten by the bug of exaggeration. This chap is renowned for sitting chest out and

solemn faced preaching to an open mouthed audience in the confines of a damp allotment shed or propped up against a bar of the local ale house or working man's club, his borrowed cigarette blanketing smoke into the room, his beer voice groping nonsensical examples how he achieved this, or he had a dog that did that, when in fact the total of his hands-on experience amounts to far less than he actually boasts of.

Then, we have the profit hunters!

The profit hunters this manuscript constantly refers to are the elite, the best of the best, men who practiced their skills consistently and with successful continuity, some whose experiences spanned decades rather than a few months or years. Where contemporaries judged their poaching, trapping and illicit hunting prowess by the number of times they had been captured and chased or by the amount of fines they incurred, the profit hunters clinically get on with the job, a tribute to cunning and a credit to guile as they mooched through fields and woods detected only by the stars.

The *Chambers 21st Century Dictionary* definition for the term profit is, "the money gained from selling something for more than its original cost, an excess of income over expenditure", but it also suggests, "to benefit from". Good countrymen not only reap larger hauls, where possible, but also profit from immeasurable amounts of excitement, pleasure and fulfilment from their sports and pastimes.

Financial gain if any is a direct by-product of their success, not necessarily the driving force, although there were those who virtually did make a living from the countryside, and there were others who poached so their families actually survived, and yes I'm talking about in the 20th century. It has been said, and documented on a number of occasions that "numbers are not everything". In most cases such a premise is fashioned by individuals who do not possess the ability or wiliness to obtain larger tallies, or, who unfortunately don't reside in a geographical location supporting large volumes of what could be deemed as quarry species. It always surprises me what people will think up in an attempt to tarnish others who have attained a high level of success, in any sport, hobby or vocation but this is life, and life my friends at times can possess all the essence of a bad sandwich.

Of course numbers are important, to a degree, their significance illustrates the success of the individual as a hunter, or if he is a dog man, the ability of his canine companions. For the individual who is the main provider for an ever demanding family, numbers ensure more food on the table.

A poacher who catches nothing is exactly that, nothing. If a professional rabbit catcher on an estate heavily infested with coney only accounts for the odd rabbit, he remains a rabbit catcher, but is he to be classed successful? A mole man having completed his task but finds nothing in his traps, and witnesses the landowner's silage fields and meadows resembling heavy plough, has he accomplished any form of victory?

Hunting accomplishments and taking wildlings are represented by what has been caught, not, what is thought could be taken, and certainly not by lame excuses by the hunting part-timers. The part-time hunter or the one for the pot man may have a place in the hunting world, however in my eyes they have only limited worth in the pages of this manuscript.

In the vocation of taking game, the profit hunter is as true an all-round hunter as the wily lurcher dog he possesses. He is as much at home with a longnet and hazel peg sticks as he is with gaff and lamp. He reads hunting situations well, seizing on opportunities to better traditional methods. Some profit hunters may very well possess Romany ancestry or analogous blood running through their veins, such a heritage that naturally dictates they will be roamers, hunters, men-o-the-fields and often possessing not just the erg to hunt, but also to have a great affinity with bird and beast, or any activities which afford solace in the countryside they subconsciously see as their domicile.

I emanate from Celtic stock and proud of it, horse thieves from Mao, ancestors who narrowly escaped the hangman's noose and fled the tender green of Ireland to the cruel red of England. The area in which my ancestors settled was situated in the north east of England, a most beautiful location, a region that would have been lost many decades to holidaying southern invaders, had a barrier of hostile climatic conditions not kept these pusillanimous intruders at bay. The terrain of mid to north Northumberland is reminiscent to the land of my forefathers, and the stunning Scottish border is no more than an echo away. A short attractive journey towards a distant horizon over magnificent countryside, peewit-guarded fields and curlew-patrolled fells, where dry-stone walls stretch ad-infinitum consolidating the entire countryside into a wonderful mosaic when viewed from somewhat higher grounds on the Cheviots, Hareshaw and Simonside.

The ancient wild lands of Northumberland may have settled down to some extent since the days when William Wallace strode its leg lashing, energy sapping heather on his quest to pillage villages along the well-heeled Tyne valley, but many areas remain relatively un-spoilt and definitely untamed, an exhilarating area of Great Britain where every variety of game-species abounds to those who know when and where to find such treasures.

It is this most beautiful setting that forms the main location-base of my book. It is these inimitable lands that have assisted in co-producing many poachers, bird trappers and night-time-skulkers over the decades. These are accomplished men, keen and always willing to capitalize on Mother Nature's over stocking, for any poacher's ability is directly proportional to the land he hunts. On this Anglo-Scottish border setting quarry species such as hare, rabbit, roe deer, pheasant, partridge, salmon and sea trout could be taken by countless methods, and by the profit hunters, in great quantities.

I am about to take you dear reader, on a series of illicit trips into these wildlands in such a way you will literally smell the innate fragrances of every Northumbrian location portrayed. You will experience the excitement that has stirred my very soul for decades, and you will touch the textures of exhilaration that my eyes have so frequently focused upon. Candidly you will be introduced to various techniques for taking an array of feather, fur and fish. You will journey as I have with some of the top countrymen of this hard, but beautiful county, at the same time being drip fed many practical aspects of their abilities, some which you may have heard of and may have even practiced, others you will have never dreamt possible.

My aim as an author, akin to Hemingway "is to put down on paper what I have seen and in some cases felt in the best and simplest way". Therefore fancy words have been cast out; styles and types of fashionable contemporary writing may have been ignored, or improvised on in an attempt to reveal a more refreshing association with my characters and their personalities.

My book is in no way set out to criticise or bemoan any hunter gatherer of today for how little they participate in legitimate country pursuits, or indeed illicit hunting trysts, far from it, many people today by virtue of personal or domestic situations obtain a great deal of enjoyment from infrequent jaunts, others, by dint of their nature or some underlying factor bath contentedly in a pool of ideology of taking only one or two for the pot, and I my friends attempt not to be a "knocker" of anyone's particular hunting kink. Everyone is an individual and should be treated as such. It is not every man's choice to trap finches gregariously feeding on thistle-clad wastelands, gaff the kings of the sea when they annually return in gangs to spawn on gravely, singing burns and streams where they were born. It may not be everyone's wish to take pheasant with air rifle and torch or wipe out partridge coveys with lamp, shotgun or nets, or to hunt in some form or guise many times a week, every week of the month and every month of the year. But it was mine, and a number of others that I have had the privilege to be acquainted with, some whose reputations will help fill the pages of this book.

The characters documented within the pages of this book are authentic, exact in every detail; only some names may have been changed at the request of individuals or their living relatives. Each method for the taking of game portrayed really works and it will be left to the imagination of you, the reader, to decide whether or not the adventures documented actually occurred.

Reiterating, my book is for entertainment, and I will endeavour to write it with all the vivid descriptive panache of a country diarist and conservationist, it was never designed or intended to be a handbook for poachers or trappers; but its content at times will highlight what unlawful hunting enterprises men can sometimes engage in.

Within the depths of these pages the answers to so many questions may also be found!

CHAPTER 1

A Quick Look Back

VENTURING out into the countryside with the intention of illegally taking feather or fur is motivated by many things, but it has been said that two of the main reasons why poaching takes place are for need, and for greed. There are also two foremost reasons why poaching should be interpreted as unlawful, on conservation grounds and because of the rich believing that it is their inalienable right that they, and no one else should have the privilege to hunt. The former I can relate to, but the latter ideology I cannot accept nor am I prepared to live with.

During more modern times poaching in Great Britain became only a transgression, seen by many as a form of acceptable social crime, nothing more than a nuisance offence. Into the millennium however, poaching became a cloaking device for thieves, a useful tool for criminals to hide behind while raiding rich pickings from farm steadings and rural homes. The match dog scene with its big money contests is also partly responsible for landowners, gamekeepers and the police rethinking their views.

Gangs of thugs tramping over fens and farmland whenever it suits them, with a total disregard to property, stock and people have driven the final nails into our sporting coffin. We are now once again on the edge of draconian laws becoming statute, with officers having the power to raid homes, confiscate dogs, cars and equipment, and English courts and Scottish sheriffs imposing massive fines and even custodial sentences to any would-be transgressor.

Illegal hunting however, with all its forms and guises throughout every corner of England, Ireland, Scotland and Wales is steeped in characters and likeable rogues, and like idiots and sluts, every village has at least one. Each geographical location possesses a Claud Greengrass type character as portrayed in the television programme *Heartbeat* during the late nineties, and almost everyone knows a man who knows a man that can supply a rabbit, hare, and haunch of venison or salmon on demand. With local heroes providing such excellent PR work for illegal taking of game, it isn't surprising why the whole philosophy of poaching tends to summon up countless quixotic images, the most heralded from the past probably being Robin Hood, taking from the rich and giving to the poor, as well as killing a few forest deer belonging to tyrant kings along the swash-buckling way.

A much later, probably more typical modern representation emphasising the romanticism of poaching is that of silhouetted figures of a man and boy treading stealthily through dew-speckled grass and mist-veiled woods, or along the edge of dense hawthorn-lined fields, a quick-footed dog running loose in front of them, while by their sides stomps an angry terrier ready to take on all-comers. The posture of the old fellow is stooped, and over his back a damp Hessian sack hangs heavy with rabbits, while nudging from one of his side pockets the white head of a tired hard working ferret sniffs the moist air.

This mind's eye suggestion of the contemporary poacher however, has never held any such romanticism for a landowner, farmer or gamekeeper; to these individuals the night time skulker or early morning moocher hits a raw nerve that no anaesthetic could ever numb. Such victims of what is now being classified as "wildlife crime" view the poacher as a thief; a vagabond who is taking something that is theirs.

History too has never viewed poaching as a minor offence, or that the poacher is doing little or no harm, in fact quite the opposite. Poaching has taken place for centuries, and during that time there have been many brutal laws with harsh penalties and punishments dished out to anyone found guilty, reflecting how serious poaching was seen in bygone times when human life, it seemed, had very little value.

The first hint of laws in England on poaching were begat at a time when the countryside and rivers literally teamed with game. There was not the populace as there is today, so the fact remains there were plenty of animals, birds and fish to go around as food sources, as well as a supply that could never possibly be drained at that time. People taking in excess of their daily requirements and possessing a surplus to barter or sell, would never have even dinted these vast natural stocks. We humans however, possess the instinct to defend what we believe to be ours, a trait evidently handed down from nature in the same way as a squirrel guards his trees, a pewit her fields and a robin his garden.

During pre-conquest England, animals were viewed basically as food or in financially viable terms. Animals belonged to whoever owned the land they were found on, as the clannish Anglo-Saxons had neither the time nor luxury for centralized property regulations. In comparison, in post-conquest England it was the aristocracy that were to own the animals, birds and fish on the green and pleasant land and they were not prepared to share. The methods in which Anglo-Saxons and the Normans viewed wild animals demonstrate elementary differences in their two cultures.

Soon after William of Normandy was crowned King of England he seized total control of these lands rich in game. William's liking of the chase, being especially fond of hunting deer, saw him destroying anything that got in his way of declaring areas as royal hunting grounds, this included villages and even churches. The king was to create a great place for deer, where it is said that 36 churches were destroyed during its conception. William applied ruthless laws that included anyone found killing deer would be blinded.

William's son Rufus also enjoyed hunting, and he implemented even more harsh penalties for anyone breaking forest laws. During Rufus's reign a poacher could face the loss of property, mutilation or even death. Written into these laws it was also made illegal to catch birds or even take wood for fires.

After the death of Rufus in 1100, his brother Henry was crowned king and by 1200 it is estimated that Royal Forests totalled 25% of the entire area of England, and of course, the cruel laws against poaching remained in statute. In Scotland poaching was also treated as a serious offence, and landowners took a dim view to anyone taking what they saw as living property to be rigorously protected. A typical punishment north of the border between the 1200-1500's would be the perpetrator having a hand cut off, or in some cases, the penalty could be death.

During Elizabethan times punishments for commoners found guilty of poaching included hanging, the stocks, branding, whipping, boiling in oil or lead, starvation in a public place and the cutting off of various parts of the perpetrators anatomy. Poaching at night automatically carried the death sentence. Taking birds' eggs was also deemed as a serious crime, and could also incur the death sentence.

During the 18th century another cruel crack by the whip of the rich on the backs of the defenceless poor, as the "enclosure" movement drove people further into a life of poverty, where wages were low and diet was poor. Wealthy British landed aristocrats began to rationalize their farms. Using new farming technology and systems of crop rotation, they forced the agrarian poor off the old village commons that now became enclosed as private property. The jobless poor ended up constituting the proletariat working class in the upcoming Industrial Revolution. Here is a rhyme that tends to sum up what the common folk of England thought of the "enclosure movement" of the 1800s:

They hang the man, and flog the woman,
That steals the goose from off the common;
But let the greater villain loose,
That steals the common from the goose.

Many people now turned to poaching as a means to survive. Fellow commoners saw these illegal hunters as heroes, and people would attempt to rescue them from the hands of gamekeepers or police, as well as intimidate those taking poachers to court. More poachers than ever before at this time were being hanged.

As time progressed, estate and landowners began to build up their game stocks, as a new breed of upper class sportsmen were prepared to pay well for the privilege to shoot, hunt and fish. This extra stocking had a knock on effect that tempted more poachers, and in an effort to fight this increase, a variety of cruel mantraps and spring guns were added to an arsenal of brutal deterrents. The purpose of these perilous devices was to break a poacher's leg, to mutilate or even kill the unfortunate victim. Poachers found guilty in court were sentenced to longer terms of imprisonment; others were transported to New South Wales in Australia.

The English game laws of 1816 limited the hunting of game to the landowners, and the penalty for anyone found guilty of the hideous crime of taking game, including the humble rabbit in this era was transportation.

As history has shown the 1816 game law certainly was partly responsible for the increase in casualties to gamekeepers and police that England was to witness, as it became the poacher's best interest to injure or even kill those seeking to apprehend them, to avoid transportation. Poaching overall became more organised, and individuals more cunning and crafty in their task

So concluding from this brief insight into the history of illegal hunting we can determine that poaching has, and always will take place. I believe such traits in the main to be partly heritable, a component of genetic make-up of the working class, or by people from various geographical locations or origins. Sometimes men can be taught the ways and external environmental factors can influence such people's abilities to a degree, but through experience it is my belief that rarely are the best poachers procured by dint of individuals jumping on to the back of a passing fad or fancy.

This, my third book, will highlight once again a particular area of Great Britain, Northumberland, natural and untamed, an ancient county steeped in history where there lies an exciting story under every overturned rock. True there are other places that's endemic populace will boast terrain at least equal to the beautiful wildlands of Northumberland, and men as strong as those up north. Scottish border men however will tell such folk, "yis, but the Romans conquered ye lot, they cud dee nowt wi us".

Many good Northumbrian poachers have been born and lived in the land beyond that I passionately write of, and the stories that follow are representative of only a few of them. The time in which these men lived was not the cruel 1500s, or the ruthless 1800s, they poached the countryside between the 1960s and the millennium. So during their clandestine outings had to cope with more than upper class tyrants, irate red-faced gamekeepers, or a big fat ear-clipping bobby on a bicycle.

Granted, brutal man traps maybe a thing of the past, but active poachers during the times I write of ran a different form of gauntlet, that of a sophisticated police force with fast cars and later helicopters to ensnare the wildlife-taking scoundrel. However, it is my belief that the principal threat to the activities of the poachers of the nineties upwards was to be communication, and I have highlighted this premise many times in the sporting press.

We have strolled into times when a farmer or gamekeeper just has to see an alien swishing a lamp on the sleeping countryside and in a short time police and helpers will infest the area like Zulus around Rorkes Drift. Bailiffs silently monitor men on salmon bulging burns or gravely river shallows with night-sighting equipment, keeping in constant communication before their well-planned trap is sprung.

No man can out-run a telephone call or outwit a short wave radio, but if the landowner, gamekeeper or water bailiff isn't aware of a crafty, skilled poacher on the land, any net to be sprung via recognisance and communication is rendered useless. The profit hunter wins the battle, at least for another night.

CHAPTER 2

I Am Just a Country Boy

THERE are many times in our lives when one is conscious that the abilities associated with youth are things of the past, a time when climbing a high wavering elm to check out the contents of a rook's nest or to leap over a flooded singing burn become sad impossibilities.

But, there is a time when youthful zest returns, rejuvenated like a Phoenix rising from the white hot ashes of the past, a personal time when sitting comfortably alone and reminiscing past achievements or what was enjoyed. My body may now show many signs of waning life, but youth remains encamped in my heart and soul to gladden me when growing old touches me with sluggish fingers.

With an easiness that comes from willing practice I vividly remember many childhood experiences. Oh how much joy and satisfaction is taken from these reveries that taunt my waking mind, exhilarating memories that haunt my dreams bringing back images and happenings that affected my early life so much, while above the dreamy lilt booms the laughter of many old friends and the whines of good dogs from the past.

The early 1960s is well remembered as the beginning, my eyes were at last fully open, a myriad of developing senses craved new experiences and my soul had already been taken over by that merciless seductress, Mother Nature.

Thinking about it I was what grandmothers and aunties would define "a proper laddy". Black face, muddy knees with a trickle of

The author and friends.

blood running through the baked hard muck and grime; time-wounded clothes that could boast a thrilling story in every split and tear.

My exciting young life revolved around being out in the fields, meadows and lush pastures, in fact staying indoors was seldom an option. When rain, that temporary incarcerator of lively children kept me confined to my room, I sat tortured by boredom, tormented by monotony while sadly gazing out of iron panelled windows like a condemned prisoner into a garden earlier baked hard by the sun. A plot, unlike me that welcomed each diamond-like droplet as its salvation. I constantly prayed for the rain to subside, and, when good fortune eventually tended my wishes, off into the street I ran like a rabbit bolting from a deadly invasion of its underground home by a pursuing mustalid hunter.

Within the confines of that other prison, primary school, one of my tasks was that of a monitor, in charge of the nature table. This I truly relished, my tutors capitalising on my obvious enthusiasm and empowering me to bring in various items of countryside booty; old bird nests, various plants, berries, hips and haws and when in season frog spawn masses and endless slimy strings of toad spawn. For this young country boy, the lessons of nature studies and football were the only education sought, the remaining curriculum I found a bore.

The weekends were my lifeline, when the tedium of the three Rs, regimental teaching regimes and stuffy classrooms could all be temporarily forgotten. Then, quality time to rummage around what this young student conceived to be a more appropriate academy of learning, a more naturally motivating college where partridge-infested fields and jay-inhabited woods took precedence over oppressive classrooms, halls and annexes.

As a product of a typical northern working class family times were hard, and although money was scarce, love, affection and happiness were always on the menu. When food was in short measure, I remember how it was the duty of my mother, the woman of the house, to go with less. My father was the worker, the head of the house, the person who brought in the wage packet, so he had to be first on the list for sustenance. We were young so we came next in the pecking order for victuals, my mother was reduced to even smaller portions or sometimes nothing at all, and this is the way it was in those early days.

My awe-inspiring parents did their best to ensure their litter rarely went without in any department. Summer holidays would never include exotic trips abroad or leisurely excursions to warm southerly

On holiday at Whitley Bay.

Me and my mum.

locations, and excuses would have to be quickly thought up so as not to look like one of the more poorer kids of the class when teachers inquisitively asked for forthcoming summer holiday destinations.

As an unmaterialistic family we settled for day trips to the beckoning north east coast. When money was really scarce it was a leisurely walk to the local beach at Cambois, building "pot pie ladies" and joyfully paddling in large warm pools of sea water left by the ebbing tide on this flat shoreline decorated with scatterings of sea coal. In more well off times there was an automatic upgrade, trips

Old school chums.

to the seaport of Blyth, a well supported beach at that time where my job was to act as a scout, looking for a gap among the holiday making families. Once a space was spotted I would wave and shout for my parents, a large heavy towel was laid on the soft sand and we all bedded down to the customary egg and tomato sandwiches. Ah, heaven. When my dad had really done some back breaking shifts down the mine this helped furnish us with a real grade A holiday, Whitley Bay, a place of toffee apples, candy floss and fish and chips. We drooled in its famous "Spanish City", where red shuggy-boats and spinning waltzers rocked and spun us into hysterical delight.

Away from the seaside we also picnicked along local midge-infested riverbanks overgrown with feral herbage, where the drifting aroma of meadowsweet acted as a most natural and pleasant air freshener, a fragrance that is said to "make the heart merry and joyful", and when smelt today, immediately delights my senses and takes me back to these halcyon days. As we sat on our grassy banqueting table sweet music was piped via an orchestra of sedge and willow warblers, blackcaps, chaffinches and goldfinches, the entire welcoming countryside treating us akin to aristocracy as we ate sandwiches, home made cakes, biscuits and drank bottles of fizzy "Muter's lemonade". We as children were allowed to run riot in such places, through leg lashing great burnet and foxgloves and we enjoyed every second of it.

An avid countryside explorer
Throughout the long, hot summer days of my youth total bliss was obtained exploring areas where heavy bumble bees lumbered over Dutch clover, rough hawkbit, common knapweed and ox-eye daisies. Heaven came in the form of warm inviting evenings when skylarks had to be practically dragged from their last encore in the clear indigo skies. Time was devoured by the mysteries of secret places where "devil birds" screamed during skimming aerobatic displays and "scribbly jacks" nested close to the ground, these were furtive spaces where my mother would never have thought of looking for me.

This insatiable appetite of countryside interests at the early stage of my evolution consumed almost every meal on Mother Nature's cosmic menu. I waded along formative years towards spotty adolescence through tinkling streams and stagnant ponds in thrilling explorations for newts, frogs and toads. Amphibian acquaintances were taken home and introduced to my parents, then housed in tall glass sweet jars and round goldfish bowls, or in a grey tin bath that when not in use always hung on an outside wall in the back yard. My new silent friends constantly impressed my dad very much, and we took great pleasure sitting together observing these beautiful creatures, but how they terrified my mother. With little wonder, as one evening around a dozen male and female crested newts escaped from the confines of various containers, the next morning there were newts everywhere, decorating the walls, clinging to cupboards, even hanging upside down on the ceiling. A few weeks later while searching down the back of the settee for money to spend at McPeaks shop at the end of our street, the decomposed remains of a newt was pulled from its last resting place.

My parents never knew what I would be fetching home next, and must have cringingly sighed, "Oh no, what's he got now" every time they saw me running excitedly up the yard, my hands stuck up a bulging jumper holding some treasured discovery, my face covered in mud, my arms and hands streaked with lines of dried blood, scars and scratches from previous bird nesting expeditions.

Some interesting finds

Every moment away from home or school was a voyage of interesting finds. Once, after a highly successful Sunday afternoon expedition to the local refuse tip at Barrington, I proudly took home a wheelbarrow load of field mice. Darting, finger nipping rodents obtained by lifting rusty corrugated sheets of iron that lay dying, half buried in grasses on these glib wastelands. My mother yelled her customary imitation of a cat with its tail jammed in the front door, squealing at me to get rid of them. This I sadly did, tipping out my scurrying friends up our back garden. A plague of mice invaded our house for months, and the snapping jaws of mousetraps echoed, "I've got one" almost every night, accompanied by the angry voice of my mother, "this is all your fault wor Bill". But looking back, it was all great fun.

Even at school my constant vigil for wildlife opportunities was evident. One of my schoolmates who always shared my enthusiasm for flora and fauna was Frankie. Although Frankie enjoyed our excursions just as much as me, he was well and truly wrapped in cotton wool by his mother, and it was alleged he was breast-fed till the age of eleven, and at playtimes when the rest of us played rough and tumble games of football and "munt-the-cuddy" or "run-a-lego", it was facetiously said my old mate took sustenance as his mother stood at the other side of the school fence with her mammary through a gap for Frankie to suckle from it.

Then age decreed we moved terrifyingly to secondary education, and Frankie on to solid school dinners, but this never curtailed the need to answer the telepathic call of the countryside.

While on a senior school cross-country run Frankie and I spotted a shoal of sea trout lying under the old stone bridge over the river Blyth at the bottom of the Furness Bank. Immediately the thought of crossing the winning line first took second place, replaced with the desire to get among these migratory fish. We waded into the ice-cold river, water so cold that it rendered any scrotum plunged into it shrivelled and empty, and a penis to disappear back into the moss akin to some form of sea anemone at the water's first icy touch. The rest of the cross country team watched in astonishment, bewildered faces looking down on the two shivering half-naked fishermen slowly striding into the river's fast-flowing attenuated channels. Our peers stoned us with various epithets of humorous abuse before they left us to get on with it. With no gaff to assist we swiped like grizzly bears at the resting silver torpedoes, managing to occasionally throw the odd fish from it's gravely retreat onto the muddy bank side. We ended up with five fine sea trout that cold, murky morning, all possessing the silvery shine associated with fresh run fish, sea lice still clinging to the skin of their hosts. Four fish we dropped off at my home, which was close to the school, and the remaining fish was given as a present to one of our favourite teachers, Mr Laverick, as a sort of peace offering just in case our endeavours had been reported by our jealous peers.

A gull in need

During one of my exciting expeditions an injured herring gull was found amid the shimmering mudflats of the river Blyth, a most productive place to seek out fishing bait, where every spade of black mud revealed rag or lug worm, and each overturned algae-covered rock exposed a green soft-backed crab angrily snapping the air with its nippers in anticipation of dextrous fingers that would kidnap it from its muddy dwelling. Returning home with the bird I discovered many times how strong and sharp the beak of these gulls are.

The convalescing creature was conscientiously fed on a varied diet of potatoes, butter beans and other left overs from our dinner plates, and even our Cairn terrier "Suzy's" dog food was not safe from my thieving fingers. The gull was coaxed back to full health over a period of recovery, sharing a wooden hutch with a New Zealand white

A herring gull on its nest.

rabbit that constantly thumped out its disapproval at the temporary feathered lodger.

When fit, my gull was reluctantly released and tear-filled eyes watched it awkwardly lift into the sky grabbing at every bit of air with weakened wings that searched frantically for a strength that had been temporarily taken away. As it slowly gained height the bird shook itself, circled to get its bearings or maybe looking to say a final farewell to the little boy who saved its life, then he disappeared towards the grey North Sea, and I returned home with my head temporarily held low, my feet kicking every stone or piece of coal on my sad journey. My body possessed a temporary unhappiness that would only be cured by the next adventure that Mother Nature had planned for me, each exciting new discovery doing its part to keep me a happy, contented country boy.

A mixed bag

In these growing years there were to be many other feathered friends that would invade my life, jackdaws, magpies, kestrels and barn owls, half feathered chicks of these were taken from nests, kept and part trained, plus adult birds captured with padded gin traps, nets and on one occasion with the use of birdlime and wands. Nests of partridge eggs where often found, the olive-green contents removed and put under "bantam or silky clockers" to act as surrogate mothers. Oh yes, grass snakes, I just loved searching for grass snakes or their soft shelled eggs in weed and manure heaps of gardener friends and local allotment holders. These are just a small number of the uncountable instances where animals and birds occupied my young life, and the memoirs of such are now and again released as I sit and ponder.

Flatty stabbing

Living in close proximity to the estuaries of the rivers Blyth and Wansbeck, an enjoyable pastime my friends and I would take pleasure in, was "flatty stabbing". This pursuit consisted of a dinner fork, stolen, nay borrowed from a parent's kitchen drawer and attached to a length of cane, broom shank or a stout hazel shaft. Then, at low tide as the steel grey water ebbed to reveal rippled sandbanks where wading birds on stilts probed and prodded for food, we would trudge

Some of my feathered friends: eider duck, gannet, linnet and an oystercatcher.

The river Blyth, happy hunting grounds.

into the shallow water like stalking herons in search of orange spotted flat fish. On seeing a fish lying motionless, these would be speared with the accuracy of an Algonquian Native, and many of these sweet tasting fish could be obtained on a good day using this technique.

Don't tell your mother

During the early 60s there was a very hard winter, and temperatures plummeted to minus extremes. A group of us travelled down the river to find it completely frozen over, from the Bedlington side to the Blyth side. This happened because at this point the river is tidal, and at high tide Jack Frost had done his icy work. It was now low tide and the river was a mere tired trickle below the ice. We walked cagily from one side of the river to the other on this new frozen crossing; in the middle we were actually stamping on the ice – what crazy things we unthinkingly engage in when we are young. We went back to the edge and did manage to break a hole in the thick ice with stones and sticks, a gateway it would seem to another planet of possible excitement and discovery.

Once under the ice we were met with a wall of eerie quietness, no eye catching movement from any living creature, no bird song detected, no whisper of the wind or rustle of trees only a hushed stillness reigned in this magical new world. With pounding hearts we cagily made for the water's edge, beckoned by its tinkling murmur calling us to come and play. Gaining confidence we waded into the shallows, flat fish were everywhere, darting then alighting on the riverbed before blending invisibly with the brown mud floor. The tips of our sticks were quickly formed into points, and we used these to spear our prey. This adventure became one of our most productive times "flatty stabbing", due to such a unique happening. I have never witnessed a second time such a phenomenon with this river stretch, and maybe it's a daring trip I would never dream of making again, as eager youth does seem to instil a drive that wards off fear and chases apprehension, where as we get older we take on shall I say, "a more cautious approach to life".

Ferrets

Throughout my childhood at least one ferret was always a resident at Châteaux Doherty; well-housed in a lined, draft-free hutch, regularly worked and fed entirely on a diet of milk-sop, with a treat of a rabbit's head, lights or liver as reward for a hard day's graft. Ferrets were continually handled to ensure the tameness desired, and my father bore the scar of a bite of a ferret in the most unusual place, under his armpit. In an attempt to show how tame he believed his ferret to be, my dad had put the creature inside his shirt, once it met with the under arm hairs it bit and wouldn't let go, my dad just stood there with a grim smile to conceal the pain from us. I too have the mark of ferret's teeth that bit to the bone on my finger, a deep wound that I stitched myself, as a matter of principle showing to my dogs if it's good for them to be stitched by me, then it's fine for me.

I obtained much delight from the sport of ferreting when I was young. Removing the scratching fearless hunter from its canvas carrying bag with my finger and thumb safely round its supple neck, and placing her at the urine smelling entrance of rabbit warrens amid local hedgerows, dense shadowy places that whispered so many secrets.

I watched in awe as the musky smelling creature paused, shook herself, and then with a slow shuffling walk disappeared into the abyss, a hemp purse net quickly placed around the hole behind her. What a buzz it is to hear, and feel the ground beneath your feet reverberating with the thunder of rabbits bolting from the approaching "mustela furo".

Most of my ferreting was done in a time long before the use of locators, an era when silence was one of the main contributing factors to a successful morning. A person who made too much noise, or lit up a fag while waiting for a rabbit to bolt was never asked to travel with the team again. No one was allowed to stand in front of netted holes, and once the ferret commenced its work, no one was allowed to move. Hand signals akin to some race course "tick-tack" man took precedence over speech, and I once saw Dennis Easton, a fellow hunter, punched in the face for spoiling a morning's ferreting.

Although I relished being out in the fields with only my dogs, ferrets and the odd magpie to converse with, I have been lucky enough to have ferreted with some great exponents of the hobby, with whom I have forged some excellent sporting friendships. I have ferreted "single holers" which amazingly yielded unbelievable numbers, worked vast warrens that took up every piece of available space on Scottish border hillsides, where an army of ferret hunters were used. I have even ferreted at night, where the essential components were a white ferret, a bright moon and an intelligent lurcher or keen whippet.

Whippets

My father in his youth was a whippet man, and imprinted in my mind are his stories of the dogs he not only ran at sweeps, but also used as hunters. These agile little dogs he called "dykebackers", and they were masters in detecting an occupied rabbit set. On finding a hole, one sniff then turning away meant no rabbits were at home, but if there was a rabbit there, the dog would sniff again, its tail wagging stiffly like a poker in the air. These diminutive dogs would then lie as meek as lambs when the ferret was busy below ground. However, when rumbling was detected an eye would half open so sunshine would not reflect in the direction of the set, ears would slowly raise so not to cause a gust of wind that would alarm a rabbit preparing to bolt and a sharp pointed intelligent head would slowly lift to expose a questioning stare. Should a rabbit get caught in the tangling purse of a net the dog would lie still, but should a rabbit break from a concealed bolt-hole, or escape from the shackles of the hemp purse net, these nippy dogs would explode into action as if fired from a punt gun, bravely running through the thickest gorse and sharpest briars to secure their prey.

18

I was never lucky enough to witness or realize the full potential of my father's early dogs, such as Bet and Kathleen's Jack, the nearest I saw of his breed were older animals, aching with arthritis and almost blind, so dad perched them on the cast iron mantle piece where they sat contentedly until lifted down.

The county of Northumberland is not only a haven for rabbits to breed and prosper, it houses a wealth of all game, and hares, although plentiful locally in those days, were very rarely taken by dogmen, and if anyone did catch one of these mammals with a whippet they were the talk of the place for months. A roe deer being taken by running dogs was a dream, and people would instantly don a face of "what the hell for?" to anyone suggesting their dogs could kill a fox. It was the abundant rabbit populous of Northumberland that were hunters' chief quarry species, mainly for food, and in some cases, as an added income.

As proficient as the Northumberland whippet and later, whippet-blooded rabbiting dogs were, they were not prepared physically for the many changes that lay ahead, modifications that would alter the face of rabbiting with dogs for many rousing years to come. These dogs had done their job, and done it well, but the step up from being a 60s rabbit catcher to a 70s profit hunter's dog was too much of a stride for pure bred whippets or many of their bastard relations to handle.

Whippets, in my part of the country, were dropped as first choice workers, resigned to a life running on the last remaining organised "sweeps", while the

Billy Wright (Spike) with two of his ferrets.

A ferret.

advancement of working running dogs, as well as myself as a country boy, moved on to another much higher level.

Bird-nesting

Of all the various forms of wildlife that completely caught my interests and attentions, it was probably Britain's indigenous bird population that could be pigeon-holed as being my favourite.

I lived in readiness for Spring time, which saw me bird-nesting, as everyone in the 1950s and 1960s possessed the wealth of a birds' egg collection, these little jewels were safely housed on beds of sawdust or cotton wool in a treasure chest disguised as a shoe box, or in the compartments of a sturdy chest of walnut drawers. A schoolboy's reputation could be enhanced to an immeasurable degree by the size of his egg collection.

When out bird-nesting my eager eyes painstakingly searched every bush, tree and patch of gorse, in fact I got to the point in this pastime where I could literally sniff out a nest. Nests that were found were very rarely stripped totally of their contents, as it had been instilled into my impressionable mind by my father that if all the eggs were taken, the female bird would impale herself on a sharp thorn of hawthorn, blackthorn or barbed wire. A misconception maybe, but one that ensured this young aspiring country boy never robbed a nest.

The smallest egg I ever possessed was that belonging to a goldcrest, a nest I remember well in a pinewood forest north of the border. On saying this however, the eggs of various tits and warblers are indeed very small in size too. The largest egg was obviously a swan's egg, and I had many of these over the years. Parent swans can be very angry when people approach their nest, and as a youngster I found the best tool to take on the day was a dog. The bonded male and female will always chase off a dog before a human, and when the nesting pair was employed seeing off any canine chum, I could get to the nest and take my reed stained egg, unless the egg was nearing its time for hatching, or as we called this, "blood dipped". A blood dipped egg was nearly impossible to blow out, and a good way of determining if the egg was at this stage was to submerse it in the water that surrounded the giant nest, if it sinks it is fresh and will be able therefore to be blown, if it floats, the chick is partly formed and the eggs were left.

During my bird-nesting life, I had also sampled a myriad of eggs from some of the most unlikely species. I remember as a youngster collecting seagull's eggs from various inland ponds, on one productive day we took 13 dozen. Some of these were sold around the streets where I lived for 2d each, others were used by my parents and grandparents for cooking, but not before being blown out into the pan or bowl and the shell kept as part of my collection. I have also tasted the delights of eggs from lapwings, curlews, partridge, pheasant, water hen, coot and believe it or not, tawny owl. The latter I remember the albumen remained clear and didn't turn white when cooked, but this had no adverse affect on the taste which resembled that of bantam eggs.

Even as my life journey slows down to a snail's pace I still bird-nest during the replenishing seasons. Today however, on finding a nest confined in a secret place no eggs are removed, only two old eyes stare in awe of the beauty lying warm and comfortable in front of them, while enjoying a feeling of sheer excitement that hasn't waned in over five long decades. Where legal I now photograph some of my finds as record photographs, and even these make the hairs stand up on the back of my neck when viewed.

Parent swans can get angry.

Bird trapping

Outside these replenishing seasons I travelled with many bird-trappers, catching a fine array of finches, seven coloured goldfinches, crimson-breasted linnets, vermilion capped redpolls and ebony headed bullfinches.

True birdmen skilfully taught me the ways of using traps, nets, wands and birdlime. I sat listening to unbelievable stories in pigeon duckets and bird sheds, often wondering whether or not the old vendors of the tales were telling the truth, or not. I was educated how to breed canaries and the importance of using related stock in good breeding plans. I witnessed the procuring of British finches and their hybrids by some of my mentors who were that way inclined, of "going agin nature", and I clandestinely visited the beautiful painted vardos of gypsies who annually took up temporary residence in various locations in our locality, some of whom would set their dogs on you or fire a catapult at your head for getting too close to their patch, while others were willing to share their bird catching knowledge with a young, eager listener.

Almost all the birdmen I travelled the local fields with are now gone, and I have indeed forged similar associations with their living

Goldfinch mating with bullfinch.

relatives. The experience I gained from such relationships left me in good stead as an aviculturalist, keeping and breeding native finches in captivity for nearly 50 years, while passing on my acquired knowledge to some of the younger generations, to ensure these ways are never lost.

CHAPTER 3

The Albino Gypsy

SUNDAYS during the exciting 1960s were booked up well in advance in the form of weekly family visits to my grandparents, where an aromatic welcome always greeted us at the front door, the smell of meat destined to be the Sunday dinner cooking slowly in its brown, savoury juices. The only occasional disturbance to this prime beef joint was a prodding fork or being lifted so a slice of bread could harvest some of that delightful "dip".

It wasn't so much the actual visit that was relished, even though I loved my tiny grandma and worshipped my jolly granddad, and their departure from this world left a void in my life that has never been filled. No, our weekend trip meant an exciting bus ride, a wondrous chugging journey down country lanes aisled with thick hedges whose shy inhabitants never seemed to resent our fleeting intrusion.

As the red Bristol floating cab double-decker bus droned past open fields, bleating garrulous sheep lazily lifted their heads from the lush green breakfast table to stare out inquisitive passengers, and cud-chewing wide-eyed cows observed us with questioning gazes. We passed slowly over the narrow stone bridge at the bottom of the Furnace Bank at Bedlington, the old bus having to almost hold its breath so it could negotiate such a fine tolerance unscathed. In the middle of the bridge the bus would almost come to a halt as the driver double-d-clutched into crawler gear with a metallic crunch,

Opposite: a stalking heron.

25

and this brief moment always gave me opportunities to scan both sides of the river to hopefully secure glimpses of a motionless heron stalking stickleback and salmon fry, a playful otter searching for an eel or a wading fisherman boasting his morning's catch towards us.

Later a new steel bridge, painted bright blue, was built across the river and during its noisy conception I must have made a small fortune running errands for 6d on behalf of the workmen for their pies, crisps and bottles of pop. The bridge updated the infrastructure from the port of Blyth, and the buses destined for Ashington, Bedlington and Morpeth began to take full advantage of this new crossing place, forgetting the old stone bridge that had been such a faithful servant over so many years. At the same time this new route opened up many more windows of opportunities for my wildlife observations on my Sunday morning travels.

There were fresh fields to scan, new bushes and trees for my keen young eyes to briefly peer into, and it was while wending along this recently established course where a newly formed gypsy camp was spotted, nestled in a small valley just off the grassy embankments leading to the bridge on the Bedlington side of the river, by the edge of a small reed bordered pond.

When I say camp, it would be more aptly described as a very small site, consisting of one canvas roofed caravan, with its wooden body pained in a combination of daffodil yellow and meadow green. The pied horse that would power this enchanting vardo stood feeding a short distance away, and two scruffy lurcher dogs strolled sluggishly, sometimes stopping to sniff the air, or to scratch the mossy ground before easing themselves down to lie in the sun. There was something mystical about this setting. An enchanting place where a whispering voice begged me to come and listen to its exciting tales, a captivating setting that commanded my eyes to stare, a situate which completely stole my thoughts as I watched absorbedly with my chubby face pressed against the cold back window of the bus until the site was completely out of view.

Although ordered never to go anywhere near, clandestine visits to the Romany setting did take place. Well, I was a young lad full of enthusiasm and seeking adventure with every step I took. This is what could be referred to as the "opposite dynasty" of my life, if my mother said go to the shop I ran to hide, if she said don't go down the burn, I went.

A gypsy vardo and fine horse.

My secretive visits to this forbidden Shangri-La were masked by trips for taking the jewels of moorhens and reed buntings that nested on and around the tarn, or during well planned outings to collect newts, frogs and toads that also found solace in this enthralling setting. Crouched undetected among the long grass, gorse and prickly brambles my wide eyes watched. So still and camouflaged was my position that a hedge sparrow probed the grass and flicked leaves up in search of insect life so close to me an outstretched finger could almost touch her rustic feathers. In another moment of waiting time a cheeky wood mouse climbed onto my foot, washed its face, and then continued its darting journey. The occupant of the vardo however remained an enigma at this point, but this was to change one Saturday morning.

From my usual seclusion, my finely honed ears detected a rumble that drifted from within the confines of the vardo, the two dogs that had been lying so peaceably on the grass arose majestically, their bulging eyes transfixed, their rat-like tails waving slowly at first, then breaking into a full gesticulate of an orchestra leader's baton as their

Reed bunting.

god stepped out on to the caravan steps and took a deep breath of mid-Northumberland air. Even the pony turned her noble head, with radar-like ears turning and jerking in every direction, its lustrous eyes reflecting past enjoyments of trotting down quiet lanes and muddy rides, her front foot scratched and stamped the ground in anticipation of being out on the road again.

This traveller that emerged was an albino, a wild man who was said to have planted his seed in many gardens of the female populace of the townships of Bedlington and Ashington.

Intrigued I attentively watched as he clambered down the stairs of the caravan, at the same time hooking his braces over each shoulder as he descended. I still believe on that morning this man sensed my presence rather than pin pointing my being there with his squinting eyes. He called for me to come out from my lair, and to show myself. Slowly my trembling body lifted from the moist grass. Brambles grabbed at my woollen socks as if begging me not to go. It was too late, the deal was done and this was to be our initial meeting and the beginning of an intriguing episode of my life that still excites me to this very day. I am a great believer in fate, and that everything that happens to us happens for a reason. Over the decades I have come to realise why the Albino gypsy was a part of my life, without this important piece the jigsaw of my life would not have been complete.

Over a period of trust building and cautious meetings he took me under his wing, much to the dismay of my parents, but during our company together he taught me a great deal in the ways of the countryside, rural lessons which stayed with me for the rest of my life. Being a proper gypsy from Romanian Zingari ancestry he knew everything there was to know about bird and beast, his nostrums, remedies and potions would have impressed Gypsy Petulengro and he possessed the uncanny ability to quiet a bad tempered horse or to make a lazy dog lively.

The gypsy's failing was whiskey and women, and this pocket emptying, heart breaking combination directly ensured he was the proud owner of an almost permanent black eye, topped up weekly on his visits to the infamous Clayton Arms in Bedlington Station, and a once full compliment of teeth that could once haul back a trotting pony were now full of gaps.

Once, on a sober day he paid a visit to my house, my father was a man of the fists and took an instant dislike to my Romany chum and unceremoniously smacked him with the type of punch I have always prayed my nose would never sample. On awaking he groggily stumbled like a punch drunk boxer to the wall of the house and half consciously began to urinate in the waste sink, the blood from his nose almost winning a competition with his piss for which could flow hardest. The Albino returned after a few weeks under the cloak of darkness and stole our hens, and a group of us repossessed our fowl back from inside the caravan a few days after they disappeared as the vagabond slept in a drunken stupor, his white head lying in a pool of lumpy pink vomit on the floor. This is the problem with these folk, you cannot show them a bird's nest for fear they return and rob it, but part of me always relished close associations with them, and to this day, still does.

My dad's, shall we say fracases, didn't spoil the relationship with my gypsy mate, gypsies take it for granted from time to time they are going to get a good hiding, its bred into them, they like it, he even said to me one day completely out of the blue, "Bye yer fatha's a hard hitter young Will lad".

The caravan that always drew me towards it possessed an unexplainable feel every time I clambered up its wooden steps. A sense of nomadic history oozed from its very core, and although the traveller lived as a virtual recluse, it always felt as if we were not alone, the spirits of arguing swarthy faced Romany's surrounding us as we sipped our snail soup.

Stacked on shelves were jars of dried out leaves, flowers, roots and barks ready for use whenever a nostrum was required. Many times I travelled the fields and woods with the albino collecting and what interesting pursuits these were. We gathered leaves including those of blackberry, dandelion, nettles and rosemary. Flowers from marigold, elder and red clover and roots of plants such as dandelion, dock and Lily of the Valley. I wasn't aware of what all these herbs were destined for, all I knew was that I was guided what to pick, and I picked them.

Outside, large black pans and tied Hessian bags hung heavy under the vardo, and a black kettle always swayed from the hook of a bowed steel hanger in the licking flames of an open fire close to the caravan. The two lurcher dogs most of the time were tethered to the back axle by a chain, then for the last couple of yards or so, a piece of rope. One dog was fawn in colour, the other brindle, both were lightly broken coated very much resembling deerhound composites, albeit in smaller, stockier proportions. The vivid pictures of this brace of lurchers remain among my first main memories of crossbred running dogs.

Often, I would borrow the two lurchers belonging to the albino gypsy, when a Brown Ale head restricted him in straightforward thinking and simple body functions. I also loaned a black cur Duke, belonging to a neighbour in our housing estate.

Duke's true owner was a widow, Mrs Purdy. The old woman would trundle down our back lane, a brown leather shopping bag hanging heavy on her arm and a stout holly walking stick clamped in her hand, the tether of a dog that looked well and truly in a huff, was held tightly in the palm of the other claw-like hand. When Duke did manage to escape his shackles however, he was transformed instantly into a constant canine component in all my outings into the back gardens of Mother Nature.

This dog was a demon ratter, the best I had seen at that time. He would practically demolish haystacks on the back of a buck rat, squeezing through cracks and gaps between bales what my ferret would have found tight. Cascades of straw would fly into the air and fall to earth like confetti before the rat's death scream rang out. Duke also accounted for many good rabbits on our moochings, and he was as sharp as any dyke backer's whippet.

A moorhen.

I recall the first time I proudly showed off old Duke to the gypsy. The brown hands of what were first and foremost hands of a "grey-koper" (horse dealer) that traded in Welsh ponies, examined every inch of my dog.

"A strong cur," he said, before going into the vardo and bringing out a box of white powder, boracic acid which he sprinkled over the dog like salt from a salt seller. His dextrous fingers then massaged the powder into the dogs coat. After what seemed like an hour I was given a brush and told to brush the dog out, which I did, and what a shine it left of the ebony fur of Duke, and the dog actually seemed to take pleasure in the whole episode.

The Gypsy's lurchers, Rai and Chavvi, when unleashed from their fetters were something quite special as workers, classy experts in taking coney, where Duke was a Ford Prefect, these were Armstrong Sidleys. They were fleeter and sharper than old Duke, and he hated them for it. His first introduction to the pair exploded into a scrap that American dog fighting specialists would have been proud of. Afterwards the trio did settle down professionally to each other's company, as if they knew what they were there for, and on a rabbiting outing just got on with the job in hand, with only the odd doggy skirmish just to key each other up.

Old travellers always seemed to have the knack of getting the best from their dogs, but not necessarily from what we would call textbook training regimes. The owner of these dogs educated me how in his youth, dog training began when the dog was a small pup, and the first step of his Romany ancestors was to tie the dog to a tree, and horse whip it till it lay cowering in its own urine and excrement. This imprinted in the dog who was the master, and when fully recovered the sapling loyally followed its master for the rest of its life, listening when it was spoken to, and doing everything it was bid. I wasn't aware of what barbarian training methods this particular pair endured during their ruthless upbringing, but it had surely been instrumental in producing a pair of dogs that really knew how to work, and what was expected from them in the fields.

The albino gypsy was quite influential in educating me on various methods for taking game, not just rabbits, and not only using dogs, some of which I will depict in later chapters of this, or maybe another book. My time with this man was a time of sheer excitement, and I remember vividly almost every episode and outing we had even many decades later. I am not finished with you yet dear Albino friend.

My last visual memory of this man was him being led away by the police with his hands shackled behind his back. For days after I visited the vardo, exercising the dogs and moving the horse to a different pitch among lush grass away from ragwort as I had been taught.

The once warm and welcoming caravan was now cold and strangely uninviting. There was no colourful fire to dance a Romany jig around while the Albino sang in strange foreign lyrics, and the old kettle no longer blew a constant soft hiss of approval at the fires gentle licking. I returned daily before and after school until one morning the vardo, the black and white horse, the two brindle lurchers and a remarkable old friend were gone.

Time has travelled much, but memories remain. Over the decades many times I have visited this setting. Oh how it's changed, but each visit is like a reunion with an old school sweetheart.

The shallow pond that acted as a saviour to so many old acquaintances is gone. Most of what we called the "valley" is now a road, but there remains a small patch of rough ground, sacred earth for me where on visits my tired eyes gently close and my mind conjures up hazy images; a beautifully painted caravan, a beckoning white haired man, a fine horse awaiting a strong pat and two lurcher dogs running towards me in anticipation of a day out in the fields.

My eyes slowly open to release a single tear that roles down my cheek following rugged contours that come with age. I think it's time to move on!

CHAPTER 4

The Nocturnal World of Longnetting

O H HOW often my mind drifts back. So vividly towards the beckoning untroubled days of my youth, a peaceful place where the autonomy and harmony sought as age steels upon me can be fulfilled in brief moments of wondrous ecstasy.

Blissfully I bathe in a lake of reminiscence. Drooling over times when the first reflections that sprung into my impressionable mind when arising from peaceful slumber were inspiring days out in the fields of my beloved Northumberland. I was rarely separated from these favourite countryside locations, and sleep, those little slices of death never won the nightly battle against being awake until every exciting thought had been totally exhausted.

Although the greater part of my existence has been taken up by this one-track mind, its consequences didn't breed me into any less of a man, or indeed any more of a specialist hunter. A motivating thirst for pitting my wits and skills against bird and beast could never be quenched by being only a hare coursing man, a lamper or ferreter of rabbits or a taker of fish from the a local burn, and its never been an option for me to be a one for the pot man. Expert moulders of men, dedication and enthusiasm, forged me into a countryside Jack-of-all-trades, where in my existence everything that took my fancy has been attempted and accomplished to some degree.

During my mid teens, a fervent time when hard alcohol and soft breasts tried everything in their powers to wrench me from my countryside interests, people often told me, "oh its just been an age thing, you will eventually grow out of it". Such statements emanating mainly from the lips of those whose abilities and drive could never match my natural adventurous streak. Yes, I did become influenced and at times dived headlong into bottles of Vaux's Double Maxum, and embraced the warmth and sensuousness of the female form with gusto, but my hunting spirit was never forsaken. Now a little older and a bit smellier, I haven't grown an inch out of being a man-o-the-fields, or losing a passion that my father genetically passed on and a vehemence that others so purposefully instilled into my very soul all those decades ago.

My hunting life may not have experienced every possible illicit form of taking game, but I have reaped rewards and benefited so much from so many, and, did have and do have my favourites. These disciplines I navigated through treacherous and difficult long apprenticeships with some great exponents and teachers at the helm to guide me. Throughout my life's voyage and even to this day my feet tramp the fields, while practicing some form of country pastime or sport. What's the point of serving an apprenticeship if you're not going to benefit from the trade?

So how and where to begin? I have decided to take you on this section of my profit hunter's journey by means of my associations with the art of nocturnal longnetting. You will be introduced to some longnetter friends of mine, kings of darkness, princes of shadows, individuals who donned cloaks of invisibility to work the lion's den of gamekeeper infested lands, locations that can be poachers' grave yards to the less cunning.

My hometown of Bedlington was blessed with more than its fair share of longnetters, men who not only worked these killing machines, but who were expert in the manufacture of them.

Harry the rabbit, a man at the top of the longnetting tree, and who grabbed every branch of learning about the sport on his ascent. Harry knew everything there was to know about using the net in the dark, he also possessed a seemingly endless supply of a new material suitable for the task of manufacturing nets – where he managed to obtain these spools of spun nylon from was a mystery – but he would always share this bounty with close comrades such as me.

Harry didn't get his knickname perchance. He was a regular provider of rabbits to so many people in Bedlingtonshire over a very long period of time. Longnetting was his speciality, as this vocation was originally fashioned as a numbers game, and Harry was a numbers man, a profit hunter. Harry oozed experience, and instilled so much confidence in me when hunting in the darkness. I never told him this, but any apprehension of hunting in places where if caught a "working over" by irate gamekeepers on top of a hefty fine could be expected was always minimised by his presence, knowledge and humour. He was also such an affable man, a definite likable rogue, and I cherished being part of his gang.

A few examples of how he attained the accolade of a rogue effortlessly spring to mind. In the local bars Harry would run domino cards, usually as fund raisers for the darts team or leek club, but there was a definite one for you, and one for me element to his crafty involvement. No one except our little group was aware of this and a good job to. The bars of Bedlington where the poachers all met were full of wild hatchet men, each one capable of breaking a jaw between pints without so much as a second thought.

Probably the one and only time when honest Harry didn't have a scam he was nearly lynched. We had been out hunting the kings of the sea, and Harry came up with the idea of running a domino card for a rather large salmon in the Percy Arms in Bedlington. There was one number left, and with no takers Harry fairly and squarely bought it himself, and it won. We had to run it again as we were so near to becoming part of a Wild West saloon brawl. Tumbleweeds rolled past as Harry donned a face of innocence and was trying to explain his purity. A rope noose was being quickly put together under a table decorated with empty brown ale bottles and big burly, hairy-arsed pitmen were already checking which chair to launch. Someone else won the salmon on the second attempt. Phew!!!

My "proper" longnetting with Harry the rabbit began when he owned a Hillman Imp, and it always surprised me how many rabbits, longnets etc could be squashed into this diminutive poaching wagon. We journeyed with great regularity over the Scottish borders to grade A hunting grounds around Grantshouses, Preston, Fast Castle, Reston and Peas Bay. These most productive hunting grounds furnished us with some phenomenal hauls of rabbits over many years, and later with the conception of lamping with lurchers the same grounds continued to afford us with unbelievable numbers.

Harry did have a farm at one time for legally obtaining rabbits in these Anglo-Scottish settings, but this was lost when accusations of sheep going missing and a drunken group of men speaking in a strange foreign tongue being seen taking sea trout ended this association with the landowner. But, Harry being Harry, used the farmer's name on many occasions when being stopped by the "feds" on the A1. Listening to and watching the prolific thespian ability of my mentor explaining to a local constable or the worst of them all, traffic police, such a blatant pack of none-truths was as good a performance as could be obtained in any theatre. Many times we sat with heads shaking or hiding in our hands amazed at some of Harry's sometimes comical answers to every demanding question thrown at him.

Once, when we had been stopped north of Belford the policeman stuck his head through the open window of the car, and was met with the stench of damp clothes, wet hemp nets and 40 or 50 rabbits.

"What the hell is that smell"? he asked. Harry sang him a tale that one of our team had a nervous stomach and had shit himself because he was frightened of the police. Well you could imagine how this was met by the rest of us; we instantly exploded into an uncontrollable bout of laughter. The policeman just turned and shaking his head said, "Look, just get the hell out of here".

Another time while being questioned at the roadside, a constable pointed to Dicky Miller who was sitting quietly in the shadows on the back seat of the Imp.

"What's the matter with him?"

Harry again got on his pulpit.

"He's been like that since he watched the film *Valdez is Coming*". Where he got some of these answers from was beyond me, but because of his smooth talk in the face of adversity we never got charged in all the time I travelled with Harry the rabbit.

Another top class exponent with the long gear was Kirky, a diminutive giggling Norman Wisdom type of chap who was once imprisoned for attempting to blow the safe in the local co-operative store offices. A net ordered from this man on a Sunday night in the local ale house would be delivered complete with bands and pins fitted by the following Saturday afternoon, with a demonstration on how to set and pick up the device on a thin strip of grass outside the pub as part of the asking price. Drivers of cars would park up to observe this spectacle, people from the bar would leave their pints to go and watch and head scarf-wearing ladies otherwise locked in local gossip turned their heads towards the leaping and jumping Kirky. Wagers were put on how long it would take this imp-like man to achieve the task.

Kirky never drove, but he was always one of the first men pencilled in when a plan was being drawn up for fourth coming longnetting outings. Some of our largest hauls of rabbits at that time seemed to occur when Kirky was part of the evening's sport.

Like Harry, Kirky was an expert in tight situations with the law. Returning from Wooler one night we got stopped by traffic police. Now, if anyone has ever been pulled over by these coppers, you will know that they are probably the most arrogant members of the British police force you are likely to ever come across. After checking our vehicle and finding over 50 rabbits the policeman asked Kirky through the passenger window, "Where did you get the rabbits?" Kirky answered with his customary giggle, "We found them dumped on the roadside sir".

How we didn't get locked up that evening was due more to good fortune rather than good PR skills.

These are only two individuals from a class of master craftsmen I will highlight at the moment, and which we will never see the likes of again. Great for the gamekeepers and the indigenous rabbit population perhaps, but not for the world of the longnetting.

Above: Kirky.
Right: *Kirky, the family man.*

Left: End pins of the long net.

Right: All the gear, longnets, peg stick and chord.

Left: The draw chord.

The longnet and longnetting

I was very young when my father decided it was time for my initiation into the nocturnal world of longnetting, where the spectral hoot of the owl replaces the raucous call of gallant cock pheasants. This sallied introduction was not to be the actual taking part of any night time jaunts. It began as any apprenticeship would, being taught the fundamentals, less exciting basic training such as harvesting straight hazel peg sticks from hedge lines and woods around the Northumberland pit town of Bedlington where we lived. My father educated me to knit with hemp cord, carefully showing the technique of a single knot that would never slip. We cut out and shaped needles from flat pieces of wood and made knitting boards that would produce the two-and-a-quarter inch mesh the Northumberland rabbit catchers preferred at that time. At this early age I would sit for hours and knit nets, finding some most interesting and at times unusual locations to practice.

There was no inside toilets in those days, our tiny loo was built onto the side of the house, with no electricity or any form of heating to make the call of nature in any way more comfortable. During the winter months a candle was often used to light up the toilet, and when the candle ran out, I would often set fire to a crumpled up page from the Journal or Blyth News newspaper stamping out every last red glowing piece of paper before I left.

Our little room was co-owned by some of the biggest spiders imaginable, and in the daytime I would become intimate with these creatures, having conversations, warning them to keep their distance. Often young Bill would run out of the toilet with his pants around his knees, cussing and cursing at a black creepy crawly that invaded those private moments.

What our toilet did have however was a nail driven into the back wall, bent over to form a hook. This was a net-knitting hook, where longnets or purse nets would hang, and a few rows could be knit while the nets' creators did their business so to speak. Toilets have many terms and names, and one such Northumberland name was a "Netty". Is there possibly some significance to this naming emanating from people knitting nets while taking a shit? An interesting thought indeed.

As a first year apprentice I was shown how to set and pick up a net, which could be 80 yards upwards in length. These were bulky hemp nets, which when wet weighed a ton and a half. I practiced during the hours of daylight, along the riverbank at the Half Penny woods, or "Happney Woods" as locals call them. After arrogantly believing this part of my training had been mastered, my dad would blindfold me, and then set me along the same wood edge, to coach my unfettered senses rather than my eyes to detect distances of how far I was from the wood edge. Early attempts saw me drifting cagily away from the wood, or tramping slowly into the trees, getting tangled up in stinging nettles, nipplewort or dock. It was a consequence of this unique

tutelage that even on the darkest of nights I mastered how to almost telepathically determine the net's setting, and would run through eerie darkness dropping the net behind me, like a coble feeding salmon nets into the hungry gaping mouth of the North Sea. At other times picking a net up in front of me that I could only see with my hands and determining where the bands lay among the net's mesh with dextrous fingers became second nature.

During my induction my trainers rarely offered me

*Above: Spike making a net. **Right:** Two-and-a-quarter inch mesh nets.*

attempts of pulling the draw cord, as in my tender years, this was a most tiring practice especially over a rough terrain of long grass and dotted patches of cotton thistles, so for this brief moment in my learning curve, the task was allocated to one of the stronger members of the team.

The area where the nets were to be used were known as "drops", and if weather conditions were correct and the expedition well conceived, there could be numerous drops done in one night. Profit hunting gangs would never settle for a single drop in one evening. The areas for hunting were well known to the longnetting team, so as not to be snagged by an unwelcome tree or nuisance telegraph pole, but a flock of sheep that had been put in the fields a few days earlier may not be so easy to prepare for. Foxes and even badgers could occasionally be ensnared in the "bagging" of the net, and many a time a hare would run the net, an occurrence where the animal would run along the length of the net with its side pushed against the mesh. In this situation you could feel it coming towards you and would take a kick at it as it shot past you in the darkness. They all count.

These nocturnal hunting trips could be preplanned to an extent, but more often than not a night's longnetting would be a last minute decision, or arrangements altered to coincide with a change in wind direction. My dad possessed a notebook, handwritten almost illegibly in his own scribble, marked with net positions, and crucial wind directions. A most useful documentation.

In my later years as a longnetter I worked rabbit-infested fields at night with some of the best longnetters in the county of Northumberland, Harry the rabbit and Kirky who I have already mentioned, but also Dicky Miller (son of the ragman in my book *A Bird in the Hand*) plus Spike, Billy Wright.

Harry knew every productive drop from Bedlington to North Berwick, and would lick his finger, point it skywards testing which way the angry wind was blowing, then, off the top of his head could tell you what drops would work best on that night.

Longnetting with my great friend Billy Wright was as much a fantastic experience as was a visit to his home. Entering Spike's palace via the front door you were immediately greeted by a museum of animal skins, trophy heads, stuffed birds and wildlife pictures adorning every wall. As a longnetter Spike saw every nocturnal outing as an expedition, and jaunts were organised with all the logistics of a military manoeuvre. There was a checklist of necessities, including food, water bottle, knife and a copy of the Journal newspaper, as Spike would often mark his territory by taking a shit, and the Journal was seen as the ideal toilet paper.

Spike's longnetting attire had been stolen from a scarecrow residing in the fields around Wooler, a most productive region in north Northumberland for game, and an area we profit hunters always referred to as "the promised land". Buttons were removed from Spike's newly acquired uniform as not to snag the net, a deep pocket had been sewn in to house peg sticks and the time-wounded coat was never washed. He liked to smell like "the fields" when out hunting, not a man with clothes washed in Daz or Omo.

Spike akin to me was a profit hunter, and I can remember him sitting drinking in the local pub with me and poaching friends on a Sunday night, Spike ready to go to work, waiting for 10pm when the pit bus to Shilbottle colliery would pick him up.

"See you Spike", we would sarcastically say as the unhappy figure slouched out the double doors of the Percy Arms.

Within five minutes the doors of the pub would fling open, and a roar of laughter would explode as in walked Spike.

Spike's hall of fame.

A good haul of rabbits.

"Damn it, I'm putting a rest day in, the cracks too good," my mate would say before ordering a bottle of brown ale.

Spike was, as I say a profit hunter, he took many fish with nets, vast amounts of rabbits and hare with dogs, he was part of a regular trio that included "Lord Ford" and "Badger Johnson" that obtained deer in numbers I have never seen any team match in my life time and when it came to big bags of rabbits, longnetting was probably his first choice. An expert longnetter, and a friend who, until now, I've never had the chance to say I greatly admired.

The net's construction: end pins

For each end of the longnet there was a metal pin, a straight piece of steel rod with a large round ring formed at one end, the other end sharpened to a point so it could be pushed easily into the hardest earth. These pins in my early longnetting days were manufactured for my dad by the friendly blacksmith at the colliery where he worked in Bedlington, and although this giant of a man had no local spreading chestnut tree to stand under, his arms were as strong as iron bands. I remember the clanging anvil chorus and the smell of red hot steel on hoof when my dad took me on thrilling visits, and how the "blackie" would lift me effortlessly off the ground with one swipe; placing me on his shoulders where no give in his shiny muscle could be detected, a solid, but most welcoming seat.

Draw cord

In Northumberland the preferred device for driving feeding rabbits towards the net was the draw chord, often nicknamed the "dumb dog". This was tied to one end of the net to one of the metal pins, then run out into the darkness away from the wood or hedge row being worked. The cord was then dragged back towards the net in an arc-like fashion, continuously being pulled and swished. This lifted any rabbits in the cord's reach, and drove them to the awaiting ambush. Shaking a box of matches, clapping hands and, god forbid, using a dog will secure rabbits, but a cord will always work better.

In my youth the draw cord, as with the metal pins, was obtained from the colliery. When winding wheels and shale heaps adorned our industrial landscapes what a source pits were for all sorts of useful items, a veritable plethora of tool supply, from Wellington boots, to snail brand spanners, from orange painted cold chisels to bow saws and axes. Every local allotment and a great number of back gardens boasted sheds and huts protected by the black and white chequered plastic on loan from the local pit, for protection against howling winds and driving rain.

Dogs and net work

My friend the late Brian Plummer in his book *The Complete Lurcher* highlighted the possibilities of nocturnal longnetting with the aid of a dog, as far as I am concerned in an attempt to create usage for the high percentage of litter wastage in his favoured first cross collie x greyhound matings, progeny that at times are both heavy and small for dogs of good all-round abilities. In his exceptional book he also mentions "Night-hunting poachers of old" supposedly preferring various hunting traits in dogs they used for longnetting. I am a man of this breed, also having first hand knowledge of many men my senior who are very much night time poachers of old. None of them would ever contemplate using any dog to accompany them on serious nocturnal longnetting outings. There are very few dogs that would be capable of such a task, and even less lurchermen with the ability to train them to the standards necessary. When it's numbers that are required on the night using a longnet or two, our canine chums would be better off left in their kennels on a warm bed of dry straw.

Longnetting is not a vocation for a "one for the pot man", although a friend of mine would run home, make his plan of attack and then longnet a local field on seeing a solitary rabbit. Longnetting is first and foremost a numbers game, exponents of the science of the longnet wishing to seize the maximum number of rabbits possible, so to do this, rabbits have to be driven towards the net, not chased in every direction.

I have heard tales of, but never witnessed a dog working effectively and more importantly efficiently to longnet. Don't get me wrong, I have witnessed dogs out at night while their masters set longnets along a dark wood edge, but a dog working well, I don't think so. Most I've observed ran about like headless chickens chasing rabbits in every direction. The ground on which we hunt can be likened to the land of make believe at times, so until I see it, I will always don a coat of disbelief. Dogs working to a gate net, well this is quite believable. There are a lot of dogs quite capable of this task, during the day and at night. I worked one particular bitch of mine many times to this, and I am far from being a dog trainer, possessing neither the ability nor the patience.

The tall tale tellers
Although the capabilities of the longnet for the taking of rabbits is renown, some people involved with its usage do, shall we say, tend to over ice their cake a bit when telling of their prowess using this device. Tales of 100 rabbits caught in one drop echo around many pubs and bars where intoxicated night time hunters frequent, but the authenticity of the statement is as blurred as the words of the club

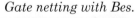

Gate netting with Bes.

CONTINUED. 1986.

1986   OCTOBER.   1986

22nd 13 PARTRIDGES (410) £13.60
23rd 11 PARTRIDGES (410) £15.20
25th 1 HARE (KIT) £7.20
      27. RABBITS (KIT 14 RUSH 13) £4.00
27th 1 HARE (PADDY) £2.60
      6 RABBITS (BES 2 KIT 2 PADDY 2).
31ST 27. RABBITS (BES 8 KIT 6 PADDY 12.)
      (TRADITIONAL RECORD) £6.00

   (37).   5 HARES (DOGGED).
(584). 117 RABBITS (DOGGED).
   (32).   8 RABBITS (SHOT).
   (10).   4 RABBITS (SNARED).
(261). 155 PARTRIDGES (410) £36.70

BES. 25 RABBITS   KIT. 2 HARES
         40 RABBITS

1986.

612   1986.

1986.   NOVEMBER.   1986.

1ST 10 RABBITS. (BES 1 KIT 2 RUSH 7) £2
3RD 34 PARTRIDGES. (410). £43.50
4th 1 HARE. (PADDY). £1.00
5   RABBITS. (BES 1 KIT 1 PADDY 3) £2.40
8th. 1 DEER. (PADDY.) £32.
     1 HARE. (BES). £2.50
     13 RABBITS (BES 6 KIT 3 PADDY 4).
10th 2 DEER (BES 1. BES KIT PADDY).
13th 1 DEER (BES KIT. PADDY) £15
     1 FOX (KIT) + (BES. PADDY) £1
     1 HARE (BES) £2.50
     8 RABBITS (BES 2 KIT 2 PADDY 4) £1
20th 7 PARTRIDGES (410) £9.60
22ND 1 HARE (RUSH). £2.50
27th 2 RABBITS (PADDY).

BES.   KIT.
     continued

1987.

1987.   AUGUST.   1987.

2nd 2 HARES (BES + BLUE 1 BRET)
4   41 RABBITS (BES 18 BLUE 12 BRET 11)
9th. 1 HARE (BES). £5.
36 RABBITS (BES 9 KIT 11 BLUE 15) £5
1 RABBIT (BES or BLUE) £10
23rd. 1 DEER (BES + BLUE)
18 RABBITS (BES 4 KIT 5 BLUE 9) £108
25th 55 RABBITS (BES 23 KIT 5 BLUE 27)
27th 1 HARE (BRET)
      76. RABBITS (BES 26 BLUE 30 BRET 20)
29th 1 HARE (KIT) £1.50
      43 RABBITS (BES 14 KIT 8 BLUE 20)
   (38) 5 HARES (DOGGED)
   (471) 270 RABBITS (DOGGED) £52
   (9) 1 DEER (DOGGED)
BES 1 HARE + 1 DEER KIT 1 HARE
   94 RABBITS   29 RABBITS

1987.

1987.   SEPTEMBER.   1987.

1ST 29 RABBITS (BES 9 KIT 6 BLUE 14)
4th 83 RABBITS (BES 14 KIT 11 BLUE 34 BRET 34)
6th 1 HARE (BES)
     52 RABBITS (BES 17 KIT 12 BLUE 23)
8th. 3 PARTRIDGES (410.)
13th. 4 RABBITS (KIT 1. RUSH 3)
18th. 1 FOX (410)
     5 PARTRIDGES (410)
19th 46 RABBITS (BES 23 BLUE 23)
25th 1 DEER (KIT) £23
     2 RABBITS (RUSH)
   (693) 216 RABBITS (DOGGED).
   (39)
1 HARE (DOGGED) 1 FOX (SHOT)
   (10) 1 DEER (DOGGED)
     8 PARTRIDGES (SHOT)
BES 1 HARE   KIT 1 DEER
   63 RABBITS.   30 RABBITS

A sample of animals caught over the years.

48

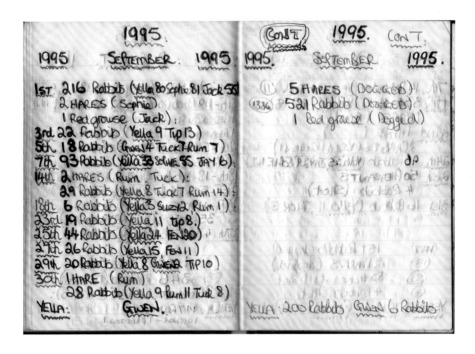

entertainer in the next room. Yes, I have been out with longnets for rabbits where we have taken more than a "ton" of coney in one night, but this was after a number of drops, and a lot of dammed hard work.

There are also those who would boast of longnetting, but who didn't have a clue about it. New fangled quick set nets were purchased from the local fishing and shooting shops and these men were instantly expert longnetters. For nocturnal hunting I did once borrow one of these so called quick set nets, and found it poor. The next day I asked the net's owner if I could remove all the little knots that secured the sheeting to the bands, the net did work better the next time out, but the material the net was made from would never be my first choice.

Nocturnal longnetting is part of my genetic make up, and the whole idea of it still holds so much excitement for me. At nearly 60 years of age a longnet still hangs on a nail in my shed, to have the odd excursion out with an old friend or two. A couple of drops and 30 or 40 clean rabbits in the bag to top our freezers up is all we go for now, but memories of the times when we literally massacred the rabbit population of Northumberland and the Scottish borders will remain with me for the rest of my life.

CHAPTER 5

Heads Will Role

ALTHOUGH there were many longnetting teams that plundered the Northumberland countryside in the late 60s and early 70s, these gangs were not as "closed shop" as the lamping poaching teams that practiced their sport a decade or so later. Yet even within these groups there were preferred members, but if one person wasn't available, I've seen us pop into the bar of the Bedlington Station working man's club, the Clayton or the Percy Arms, and practically press gang someone to make our number up with stories of riches beyond their wildest dreams.

One dark winter's evening, with a bitter easterly blowing we needed an extra man. On this occasion we called into the infamous Clayton Arms, where a nightly assemblage of rogues and vagabonds gathered. Eyes akin to those of crows and ravens stared as we entered this bandit's lair. Uncomfortable thoughts of hyenas, jackals and vultures passed through my mind as I hid in the shadow of Harry the rabbit.

"Anyone want to go longnetting?" Harry called. An explosion of silence ripped through the smoke-filled room, an intense quietness that froze the potting of the black ball, the hitting double top of the dart board and the placing of the double six domino. Inquisitive heads turned towards our small scruffy band. Then a voice answered.

"Al gan." It was Geordie Lawson, the hardest man in Bedlington. Now don't get me wrong, we weren't too bothered about taking this man mountain, in fact this could have its advantages, but it also had its drawbacks.

Geordie had been a protector of all of us at some point in our lives over the years. He saw himself as the boss of this pub, in his dreams the "Clayton Arms hero" Geordie was a hell of a fighter, and my dad once told me how Geordie would fight grown men when he was only 14 years old. At the miner's picnic in the early 60s, goaded into a boxing booth Geordie knocked the semi-professional boxer out with one punch. As a fighting machine he was like a windmill, his arms lashing out in every direction at a speed the naked eye had trouble keeping up with. Geordie was fearless, and would take on all comers, any time any where. I am so proud to have bought a pint and shaken the hand of the man that would fight any man in the world.

One night when walking back home to Ashington from a night on the beer in Bedlington, I got jumped on by five lads. The next night Geordie seeing my scars asked what had happened. A couple of the lads were known to me, and I mentioned that they drank in the Lord Barrington pub in Stakeford. Geordie practically picked me up and made me go with him to reap revenge.

Standing outside the pub's narrow doorway, Geordie said calmly.

"Just point them out and get out of the way." I did and within less than a minute of entering the pub there were a pile of bodies lying in a groaning heap on the polished floor in front of the fine oak bar. Geordie strode past me still psyched up whimpering like a dog that's just had a scrap, the fire of hell still burning in his eyes and saliva drooling from his parted lips. Geordie, a great man to have on your side.

The main advantage of Geordie becoming a temporary member of our gang was that no gamekeeper would dare come near us. The disadvantage, he had not been longnetting before, so a task befitting with his abilities would have to be found. God had blessed Geordie with the fighting prowess of a Spartan warrior but without acumen. Dicky Miller, one of the other members of our team that night, however came up with the ideal answer. When the rabbits were in the net, Geordie could go along the net and kill them. Sorted!

"Just twist their heads and pull," I remember Dicky coaching our newest recruit.

With big Geordie riding shotgun, apprehension waned and audacity grew with every mile we travelled. Into the lion's den we rode. Powburn, a village south of Wooler, the mere name of which would fill any illegal hunter with dread, a "poacher's graveyard".

Sometimes two longnets were used!

Our car was parked in the council yard on the north side of the village, and we cut across the main road and under the bridge that spanned the river Til, a river that during the spring would sing a soft lullaby to nesting dippers, sandpipers, snipe and oystercatchers. During the autumn months the burn sang a different song, one of thunderous roars and challenges that enticed spawning salmon from the Tweed to negotiate its fast flowing channels, but that's another story.

We crept low along the deep bank side using the river's noise to disguise our presence, crouching so low at times we actually had to wade through the icy waters towards our destination.

On reaching the fields where experience had taught us the rabbits would be feeding out in great numbers, we clambered onto the bank side akin to a family of otters and next to where the hedge that acted as a partition sloped towards the icy Til. Harry quickly and silently got the nets ready, as tonight we would be using two 80-yard nets rather than one 100 or 120-yarder.

The end pin was skewered into the soil already hardened by Jack Frost's presence and Harry set off with the nets, feeding out the first

Spike pegging out a longnet.

of the killing machines as he ran. I held the net in one hand, pulling it towards me, then within a short time the feeling of the net being pulled violently dragged my gripping fingers, this was Harry at the other end of the net, telling me it was time for my task, to peg the net. With the net in my hand to guide me I entered the arena of darkness, running close to the ground akin to a hare belly running in an attempt to flee undetected from a hunter's gaze. To my left the dim shadows of the hedge and to my right a sinister murkiness with eyes that watched my invasion of the sleeping grounds.

A few yards in and the first peg was fixed. First I felt for the thick banding cord of the net, this was pulled over my head as I had done many hundreds of times before, allowing me to work unhampered by the net's dense bagging as I twisted the peg stick around the bottom band before shoving it firmly into the soil. Once secure, the top band and sheeting of the net was removed from my head, the top band wrapped around the peg stick and that was that. The first of a number of hazel sticks in place, the net was pulled taught as I ran to the next position for a stick to be placed, adjusting the sheeting of the net as and when required. All subsequent sticks usually have the bands wrapped around the peg sticks only once, but this can be altered as and when necessary to twice at times to maybe tighten up a droopy net.

At the end of the net I felt the iron loop sticking in the hard earth, and a yard further, another end pin of the second net, already being laid in position by Harry, the master craftsman. My work again began, no time for rest, no time to

The late Dicky Miller and friend.

*Above: Harry the rabbit on the North Sea. **Below:** Harry pulling a pint.*

ponder, as any second Dicky would be starting to employ the draw cord to drive the rabbits to the nets. I knew my job would have to be done as quickly and efficiently as possible, it was a race against time now, and I crossed the finish line with the dark figure of my mentor waiting crouched by the end of the net like a castle gargoyle.

I took my place by the side of the man that had shown me much in the way of longnetting over the years, my hand resting on the top band of the net, in anticipation for the knock, a feeling akin to the bang like a bite of a fish on a line, letting me know the net was now doing her bit for our evening's work.

Suddenly a quick succession of knocks could be felt on the net, two, three, four then I began to lose count. At this point we let the rabbits hang themselves, staying positioned like eager retrievers waiting to pick up. Then, a screamer, a rabbit fairly close to us that wailed like a Banshee as she tried to push and pull from the net's grip around her neck, her teeth chewing and biting at the net in an attempt to free herself. I bolted from my seat and quickly dispatched the noisy creature, leaving it hanging in the sheeting of the net then returned quickly back to Harry.

Again we played the waiting game, until emerging from the darkness we could here the swish of the cord being swept across grass in front of us, a unique noise, an exciting noise imprinted in my mind over so many hunting seasons. Then, the first sign of Dicky silhouetted against the darkness. It was time to make a move, and I began to walk the net, killing any rabbits I came across. I hoped that Geordie would be doing the same coming from the other end of the other net, and at some point we would meet up.

This is the thing with organised longnetting teams, profit hunters, everyone doing their respective tasks to ensure maximum efficiency. In my head I knew Harry would be following me removing the rabbits, now still and lifeless from the net. I got to the end pin, no Geordie. I decided to double back and give Harry a hand collecting the rabbits. Dicky, who had been at the end of the net where Harry and I had been sat, emerged from the other end of the nets. How the hell did he do that? I thought to myself. Dicky's voice was masked with laughter.

"Wait till you get down there," he said, pointing in the direction where Geordie was.

Harry and I carried the still warm bundles of rabbits, Dicky got on with rolling the draw cord skilfully around his hand so that it would be ready to roll on our next drop, shaking his head and chuckling as he worked. We got past the middle point where the two nests met. A rabbit was still in the net, hanging lifelessly, but without its head. Rabbits a little further down the length of the net had been removed, and were lying belly up as required, but all fully decapitated.

Geordie appeared out of the darkness, quite proud of his maiden longnetting achievements. His large and sinewy hands that when clenched had broken so many jaws in the past were so powerful, that his twist and pull was a bit too strong for the supple necks of the rabbits.

Many heads rolled on that night, literally.

CHAPTER 6

The Loneliness of the Long-distance Longnetter

BEING out hunting in the dead of night has always held a certain fascination for me. Treading stealthily on a carpet of sombre dead leaves laid expertly over damp sodden ground, while immersed in a mysterious world with the Great Bear and Cassiopeia as my heavenly companions is an experience that yields me so much satisfaction. The countryside I arrogantly see as my own not only looks different when night time draws its velvet curtains, but it also feels so different.

By dint of nature and genetic make up I am first and foremost a loner, but where necessity decrees others as company on a night time hunting foray, then so be it, and I have always had a bank of others to rely on, but overall, I much prefer my friends to have four legs rather than two. Dogs will not purposely let you down, they will not talk about you behind your back and they won't run off with your wife. Dogs have assisted in securing many rousing times over a great number of years to look back on, and one particular event I would like to highlight in this chapter.

During the late 90s an evening's sport was almost curtailed when my lamping partner was struck by a horrendous bout of influenza, yes that dreaded man-flu. I had been on edge all day, excited by a southwesterly wind that grew stronger as the sky got darker. My battery bubbled gently as it approached full charge. My Yella, a lurcher with all the sensitivity of a dog and a human being's perception, constantly stared at me in anticipation through the bars of her run.

That was it. I decided to go it alone, to my wife's words of "you must be mad". Mad I am, hunting mad.

To add confirmation to my insanity, I decided to also take one of my longnets. The wind direction was such that one or two good "drops" might be obtained, before working other fields with my lurcher and lamp. I come from a family of longnetters, also from an area of Northumberland being one of the last bastions where this activity is performed as it should be in the traditional nocturnal way. I have dropped a net alone many times so this would never be a problem, but I am the first to admit, it works better when there is a team of two or three.

I chose an 80-yard net for this excursion, collected my hazel peg sticks and roll of draw cord and loaded them into the back of my Daihatsu Fourtrak. My lamp and battery, and a lurcher that never barked or let me down were put in the front.

The journey to my hunting ground took approximately an hour and a half, driving over the Scottish border deep into this history-steeped land. On reaching my destination I parked behind a mixed wood of ash, larch, birch, and a few Scots pine. The strong wind roared loudly, swirling violently around the treetops. This was truly a textbook night for hunting of rabbits I thought to myself. For a brief moment I pictured my friend lying incapacitated in a stuffy bedroom, drinking Lemsips while I was living a dream in a setting that yields so much contentment. Ah well, off to hunting.

Yella was keen and excited, but eventually accepted she wouldn't accompany me on the first part of the evening, when I told her in a voice of firm grandiloquence to "stay and lie down". The dog at a snail's pace circled and lay in a spot so small a ferret would have found difficult to fill. Later, when common speech and Geordie slang are restored, Yella will know it is her turn. But for now dear friend, it is time for you to rest.

All my longnetting components were collected, the vehicle was locked and the keys hid behind the back wheel then I headed into the shadows, and a muddy ride that split through the wood. My eyes strained, searching for any glimmer of light to guide me. Then, in the distance through silhouetted trees a gap that indicated the entrance of the fields. If the farmer hadn't changed anything, the old wooden gate would have only a rope loose holding it closed.

Once in the field I quickly twisted free the first steel looped pin of my net. This I drove deep into the firm Scottish soil. I ran stooped, at

the same time allowing the net to flow behind me off the second pin. The wrath of the wind was blowing off the field towards me, disguising my presence from even the most nervous rabbit, and I quickly reached the end of the net. I tugged on the net taking up any slack, and drove the second pin into the ground.

This is where I really miss having someone with me. At this point the net would have been already pegged into a position where it would be effectively killing. Being alone, I would now have to do this task, and as quickly as possible.

My hazel peg sticks were held in a home made "quiver" inside my trench coat. I twisted the pointed end of the first stick once around the bottom band of the net and shoved it down into the ground. The top band of the net was twisted around the top of the peg in the same fashion. This procedure was continued at intervals till I reached the end of the net. This was the net set. The reader should be aware; this was being done in total darkness. No light to guide the way, or hammer to drive the peg. Experienced longnetters have the ability to do this, using finally honed senses educated over many years.

With the net set, the draw cord was attached to the first pin. I then ran up the plantation, then out into the field away from the net, swishing the thick cord behind me. The aim here is to run in an arc, making back towards the net. Although nothing could be heard but the anger of the howling wind and the call of a young cock pheasant that had been awoken from his slumber, I knew rabbits would now be hitting the net.

I reached the plantation edge and instinctively found my net. Traveling furtively along it I made out the white belly of a rabbit caught up in the net's sheeting, quickly dispatching it without removing it from the net's grasp. I moved on to the next rabbit ensnared in the clutches of the 80-yarder, and repeated this to the end of the net. That was it, only now I could take a well-earned rest.

After a short while the complete haul was removed from the net, a total of 18 good, big clean rabbits. The speed and fervor associated with setting a longnet is never required when picking it up, unless hunting in the lion's den where vigilant gamekeepers maybe bedded down or do spot checks protecting their birds from an old wily fox that has been causing them to stir from their sleep. This net has done her job well, time to plod back well laden to the greeting of my old lurcher and let this part of the countryside return to peaceful slumber.

When back at my vehicle, Yella was let out to clean herself while the rabbits were sorted and my longnetting gear stored. An ear was removed off every rabbit so it would be easy to tell later which were the dogged rabbits, and which were clean netted ones. Yella, although a great rabbiting bitch, does like to munch on a bit, especially with the rabbits she takes early in the night, after 20 or 30 however, the enthusiasm of her strong jaws wanes and the latter rabbits on an evening sport are never so badly marked. When ready my canine chum rode shotgun as I drove to another part of the estate, which for the moment lay quite unruffled and undisturbed. It was now going to be Yella's turn to exploit the excellent hunting conditions and large rabbit numbers.

In the first grassy field that eventually met up with heather clad grouse moors, many good rabbits lay feeding. Yella, my oldest lurcher picked her first five rabbits up after they had risen from their seats and before they could get anywhere near the sanctuary of their cavernous homes. I never count the ones that get away, and in the first half an hour this old girl had caught 16 rabbits.

When lamping rabbits, it's always favorable to have ideal weather conditions, but they are not as critical as when on a longnetting expedition. The aspiring lamp-aided hunter can afford to make an amount of misjudgments, noise, illuminate your path through dense shadows or twang the odd wire of a fence and still have a decent night's sport with your dog. Do any of these when longnetting, and that's your evening spoilt.

With my dog in her usual top form she took another 20 rabbits covering a number of fields and even some taken on the heather, burn off and with new tender shoots already exposing themselves through the old plants' tangled, charred remains. This is the benefit of possessing an experienced, seasoned campaigner. A less experienced dog may have only accounted for a fraction of this old girl's total, and possibly done double the work to get them.

Finally and sadly it was time to leave this Anglo-Scottish setting, having tasted the enjoyment of both longnetting and lamping. My two favorite pastimes employed for securing large numbers of rabbits had once again helped put the light back into my eyes and a smile in my sole. Without such hunting activities to quench my hunting fervor I would have only lived half a life.

Driving south along dark winding, narrow country roads towards the A1, my headlights exposed some of nature's night time skulkers.

A fox attempted a game of dare, trying to cross the road in front of my vehicle, but wisely decided to go back to the sanctuary of the damp grass verge. A barn owl, that spectre of the night glided out of the darkness and veered broadside allowing me a fleeting glance of its bright white undercarriage before disappearing back into the dark abyss.

Suddenly a feint glare of approaching lights glinted through trees and bushes that aisled the narrow road. The mild orange glow exploded into full beams of bright white light as a vehicle approached and passed.

"Bugger," I uttered out loud, it was the local police.

Old Yella, detecting a note of concern in my voice, rose quickly out of her warm lair, her wide, lustrous eyes scanning the darkness.

"Its ok old girl, I think we are going to have company."

Checking my rear view mirror an intense red light vibrated in the darkness, it was time to put the beats in, and my foot stamped the accelerator pedal flat to the floor. Now these old Daihatsu F50 were quite nippy for a 4x4, much faster and fleeter than the old Landrovers I had traveled aboard in the past, but to outrun a modern police vehicle, no chance. I quickly searched for ideas, for excuses to give why I should be out in the dead of night with a car full of dead bunnies, a lurcher dog, lamps and longnets. Visiting a relative, no. Testing the vehicle after a major engine overhaul, no and saying I was out looking for permission was also out of the question. I decided to use my cloaking devices, switches that I always added to any poaching wagon I owned to turn off tail and stop lights. After a few more bends in the road I braked hard and turned into what resembled a farm drive, stopped, switched the engine and head lights off and waited.

Yella paced back and forth over rabbit carcasses and nets, believing she was going to be let out of the vehicle on the back of a fleeing roe deer as she had done so many times before in similar circumstances on our homeward journey. As I thought, the police car had turned around and was now in pursuit of me, going past my hideout at a fair rate of knots; the hunter was now the hunted, a type of hunting that I have never profited from.

I sat pacifying my dog, letting her know some of the ideas of what my next step would be. What seemed like an eternity passed, and it was time to make a decision. The motor was restarted and the vehicle reversed on to the main road. This is where I made my biggest mistake of the evening. I could have gone the way I came from, and went back via a longer route over to Grantshouses and down the A1, but, I opted for the police car being so far in front they would have given up the chase and left for other things on their shift.

Again I traveled along the winding roads towards the village of Chirnside, confidence overtaking any apprehension that may have clouded my mind only minutes before, until I went past a parking place and in it was a police vehicle, lit up only by side lights and an orange glow of the interior light illuminating two figures sitting in the front seats. The lights went to bright white lights, and then joined by flashing blue lights, time to get that book of excuses ready.

I pulled over and stopped. One policeman to my window, the other checking my registration, tyres and tax disc.

"Was that you back there," the policeman asked in an authoritarian but polite Scottish accent. No good denying the fact I thought to myself.

"Yes, I stopped for a piss," I replied.

Now when being stopped by the police in such situations, I have remained unscathed over the decades by following a policy of eating

The author and Yella.

humble pie, not being cheeky, facetious or in anyway aggressive. Tell the officers what they want to know, not asking them if they should be out catching real criminals and the likes, they are doing their job, the same good coppering that caught the Yorkshire ripper. However, in the past I have been stopped by some really nasty pieces of work. Traffic police, for example, and one individual that had me pinned across the boot of my Vauxhall Viva by my throat, how can one keep one's cool in such times of adversity? But you do.

Then came the question I was dreading. "So where have you been Mr Doherty."

Eggs or chickens here I thought to myself.

"Out for some rabbits."

The other copper shone his light into the back of the vehicle, greeted by a lurcher with a frown on her face.

"Bloody hell you've got everything in there, dogs, lamps and nets. Do you always travel alone?"

"Sometimes have a mate with me, but their lass wouldn't let him out tonight," I replied jokingly.

Details came back to them that I was who I said I was.

"So its rabbits you're after Bill?" I was now on first name terms, always a good sign.

"Yes, bunnies only, not deer, no fish, no birds."

I think the pair were somewhat impressed that I was alone, and I've always thought to this day, had there been a few of us in the vehicle, they would have taken a different stance on the situation.

"You should ask for permission, I'm sure some of the farmers up here would let you on for rabbits," one of them said.

"I've tried in the past matie, but as soon as I say I'm from Ashington it puts them off. There's a lot of idiots down our way that spoil it for us genuine rabbit lads," I said. "Do you know of any landowners I could try," I asked. Always a good switch of psychology this one.

"Not really, just get on your way, and think of what I've said about getting land, because if we stop you again we will do you for poaching." He gave me a HORT 1 form and kindly explained what I should do with this, after asking which police station I would like to produce my documents at.

"Cheers matie," I replied, and we were on our way again

"There now Yella old girl, that's the way to do it." The dog detected a less stressful tone in my voice and her tail wagged, she stared at me with intelligent eyes, her ears pinned back to her smooth black head and her tongue lapped at my face, gently she squeezed through the gap in the seats circled and lay down.

The next day after work saw me visiting my ailing friend, animatedly telling him of my exploits and the number of rabbits caught. If only it were possible to bottle the effect of our conversation as a medicinal curative. Never has there been a quicker recovery from the dreaded man flu.

Batteries were recharged and we, yes, we were out again that night. As my wife constantly says, "mad".

Over the seasons I have adopted the ploy of taking both dogs and longnets on nocturnal hunting expeditions many times, usually with decent results, both with a friend, and by myself. However, as I've already mentioned in pages of this book, I would never consider using the two together. Longnetting efficiently with the aid of a dog is only for dreamers. It can, and probably has been done in the past, however not to the degree as these fantasists would have us believe. To obtain the best results, the profit hunters tend to keep them both apart!!!!

CHAPTER 7

Partridges

WALKING wearily by fields where once my legs so tirelessly wandered, I stop for a while to rest my enthusiasm, a passion for the countryside although remaining supercharged after all these years, no longer possesses the sturdy chassis to carry such a heavy power unit. The purpose of my short break however, is not only respite for tired muscles and the pains of sciatica, it is an opportunity to become intimate with what Mother Nature has on offer. We townies relish journeying to alluring rural locations to stare through nature's windows, steeling unique glimpses of all mother's children joyfully playing in their natural playgrounds, but if we sit long enough, many of these remarkable characters of the natural world will come to visit us.

Pensively I gaze across fields of winter wheat swaying under the gentle breath of the wind, creating constant rippling waves that magically sail across the land with perfect continuity, while the trees that tower above me dance to the rhythm of my daydreaming. Suddenly my old, yet keen eyes spot the raised dark heads of a family of grey partridges, and excuses to remember my guilt of a time when the profit hunter was partly responsible for drastically depleting these local stocks, comes flooding back on a cascading waterfall from the past. My eyes slowly close leaving behind a hopeless maze of worries and woes, following a track into my daydreaming discovering a magical world where spoken words find it difficult to survive.

These local fields nestling in the lower-lying lands of mid-Northumberland have always supported good stocks of this small, but pugnacious game bird. Dense hedges circumnavigating the birds' chosen grounds provide first-rate breeding accommodation, and a monogamous partridge pair will scratch out a hollow under a bush or amid long grass for a single brood of between 10-20 eggs. It is the female only that incubates, but both parents are gallant in defence of their chicks, and have also been known to feign injury to lead away potential perpetrators and trespassers from their domain.

The partridge family also have many other problems to contend with for their survival. These are ground nesting birds and depend to a large degree on camouflage for their existence, whether it be parent birds lying tight amid grass, or eggs and chicks hiding so as not to be spotted by mammalian opportunist thieves such as hedgehog, fox, rat, mink, stoat and weasel. Feathered marauders including magpie, jackdaw, crow, rook and gulls will all do their best to seek out and destroy partridge eggs or families. The weather can also have a disastrous affect on the partridge populous, and a wet June will decimate newly hatched partridge chick numbers just as much as any four-legged or winged predator.

The partridges being observed scraping out a living are a family covey, soon to disperse as the warmer months of spring approach; then as the green points of daffodils probe through the yielding soil each young individual will locate a mate to spend the rest of its relatively short life with.

For the table my taste buds have always found the partridge to be far tastier than their larger game bird cousin the pheasant, or indeed, red grouse. My preference is backed up through comparisons between partridge and pheasant prices brought in via a game dealer, which have always seen partridge prices being much higher than pheasant. What is offered at the game dealer for partridges rarely suffers the assured dramatic drop that occurs once the respective shooting seasons begin. The respectable price tag that the game dealer suggests for pheasants in September can plummet by 75% or more within a few weeks once initial required numbers have been met. Partridge prices do peak and trough over a season, but never to the same extent. So for any aspiring profit hunter, the diminutive partridge maybe the better option, financially, and taking them can be a very lucrative pastime indeed.

From talking to old poachers in the past, or when reading a variety of sporting books and articles written by some most knowledgeable authors, these have revealed various methods for the taking of partridges, mainly techniques that capitalize not only on the birds' trait of living and moving about in large groups outside the replenishing seasons, but also in the way they fly. These birds have short tails, not long rudders like those of pheasants. Where pheasants can take off virtually straight up through dense undergrowth or between tall trees that arch over forest rides, partridges are a bird of the open fields, and always take off low to the ground in heavy rapid flight, rising just enough to clear hedges or stone walls. This makes them able to be not only shot akin to every other game bird in its class, such as red grouse, but also to be successfully netted.

As a lad I remember my father hunting partridge with the aid of nets during the daylight hours, and also later on when dusk deepened into darkness. These nets would be lofted above the tops of thick hedge lines with the use of poles. If employed through the day, the poaching squad would have to flush the birds to lift in the direction of the ambush, and ensure that the birds flew that way. It was at night however when the technique worked best, here a number of tilly-lamps were often positioned behind the net to attract the startled birds. My father's team consisted of three individuals, two men to work the same draw cord used for nocturnal rabbit longnetting, each man taking an end of the thick line to drive the partridges to the nets, swishing the cord across the field.

The third member of the team would stay positioned behind the dense hedge, his wide eyes twinkling from the flickering lights of the lanterns as he waited for the birds to hit the net.

The knack was to have the cord forming an arc between the two men, not taught like a tightrope. Partridges have finely honed senses of hearing, they will detect the walking people either side of them and will be very wary of these alien noises. Then, when they become aware of the noise of the swishing cord coming towards them this will be all too much, and will usually take off forwards. Partridges packed tightly in a covey when the weather is cold may have to be practically nudged up by the cord at times, and I have known the cord to go over the top of a really tight squatting group.

Later in life my profit hunting team also used such nets, lanterns however were not part of the tools of our trade. Good hunters can adapt or improvise on traditional methods for taking game, and acknowledge that the environment itself can be a useful component to aid success. Lines of distant street lights, the powerful floodlighting from the likes of the local Alcan smelter plant or Blyth power station gave us the brightness we needed and what spooked partridges flying in the dark would use to guide them. Our nets where positioned as in nights of old, behind suitable thick hawthorn hedge rows that would be in the birds' flight path towards these helpful illuminations.

No matter when these nets where used, it became obvious that an amount of homework would be necessary to enhance success, such as observing where the coveys where feeding during the day, their preferential roosting fields and there preferred flight path when lifted. As a lad I would often do this reconnaissance, treading on moist land, my legs sprayed with shiny droplets as I passed silently through long grass. Trees and bushes still wet with morning dew acted as my camouflage ensuring that the coveys could not observe my gaze, then I would excitedly run home to inform my dad. It is this "knowing your quarry" that assists in reaping greater rewards in the long run for all forms of hunting both legal, and illegal. Even in later life, daily reconnaisance missions would be done before any night time vigils began. Guess work is only a minor part of a profit hunter's armoury.

As a profit hunter my preferred method for taking partridges was with the use of gun and lamp, and this is one of those rare situations where I have poached using a gun, except for a decent air rifle, as I usually hate guns in any form or guise. On my earliest outings on nocturnal partridge hunts a firearm was borrowed from my cousin, an old Cowey 4.10, dropping it off to its rightful owner when the illicit foray was complete, usually leaving it in a pre-planned situate, in a coal bunker, outbuilding or outside toilet.

Shotguns were very easy to come by at this time and not only from local gunsmiths and sporting shops, these weapons could be obtained via catalogues where the customer could pay a nominal weekly payment. A friend of mine did this, buying a single barrel Baikal. The gun was delivered on a day he wasn't at home, and the postman left the parcel in the coal bunker. On the same day as coincidence would have it, a supply of free coal from the pit arrived and covered up the delivery. After a few days of thinking he had not received the order, the company was contacted, and another gun was sent out. In a few weeks, when getting a shovel of coal for the fire, the first gun was found; my friend was now the proud owner of two guns, for the price of one.

Even post-Hungerford, a floater 4.10, 12-bore or .22 long-rifle could be fairly easily obtained. A visit to one of the hard working men's clubs in Ashington saw me securing a Spanish double barrelled 410,

A grey partridge.

for the pricey sum of £20. This "El Chimbo" folded up nicely so to be concealed in the most limited of spaces. I sought the services of a local joiner to make it a "skeleton butt" akin to the guns I remembered standing quietly in my parent's kitchen when I was a lad. This was a hammer gun; chambered to take three-inch magnum cartridges, a most impressive little gun indeed, and a tool that served me well in the time I possessed it.

On countless occasions my wanderings have taken me unaccompanied into the local fields in search for game birds, or with one of my dogs to keep me company, and sane. The shooting of the gun while at the same time operating the lamp, whilst not being impossible, can be exceedingly awkward. So for best results this is a task for two people, one to shoot and the other to scan the fields with the beam of light. It is also another set of eyes to keep the vigilance necessary to go relatively unnoticed.

Forays took place as soon as it was dark, so the job was completed by around ten o clock. This ensured getting back home at a sensible time, or if the conditions were favourable, a lamping excursion on rabbits with lurchers could follow, at other times of the seasonal calendar, a trip to gaff the kings of the sea in local flooded burns could take place afterwards.

Partridges roosting at night are rarely found in stubble or grass fields. I'm not for one minute saying that they will never use these environments as their divan, on occasion they probably do, but for the aspiring profit hunter they would be more difficult to find, and most coveys would actually be discovered as they are lifted under furtive step. When out for these birds, we seldom scanned anything else but recently tilled or newly sewn fields or those with short young plants just peeping through.

Flat tilled fields are much preferred by these birds, a shallow hollow is quickly scratched out as a mattress, and the whole group then settles down. Each individual will take it in turn to be on the outside, facing towards the open field. These sentry-birds quickly assess any danger approaching and will warn the rest of the family and the whole group will be ready to explode into flight. If this does happen and the main covey is split, the birds will call to each other in the darkness and in most situations they will once again regroup and form the main covey.

When scanning a tilled field with a high-powered lamp for partridges a covey will resemble a black patch against the grey ground, and as a tip from my mentors, every dark patch should be investigated, as the bright eyes associated with lamping rabbit are rarely if ever seen. If the distance of the group is not too far, then the lamp is left illuminated and the covey walked up to, and on getting closer the colours and markings of the birds will become more evident. On a number of occasions coveys were detected so close, we had to actually step a few paces back to get the shot we wanted to maximise the spread of the load.

One of my most productive nights for taking roosting partridges came quite by accident. It was one of those hunting expeditions when everything went right, and success was arrived at via a most unusual colleague, snow.

Our evening began slowly in fields close to the river Blyth. Five star partridge ground, level fields circumnavigated on all sides with dense cropped hedge, with only the occasional gap for poachers and bird trappers to use as doorways on their crafty ventures.

Suddenly the dark sky that had given us an ideal cloaking device from unwanted onlookers took on a lighter tone, shadowy darkness drifted to sinister grey, then to luminosity that suggested snow was about to pay this Northumbrian setting a visit. Into the backside of the hawthorn hedgerow we slipped, taking refuge from the driving snow. Luckily this initial deluge was short lived, but it did have time to leave a deep ermine blanket as its calling card. Our first thought, well that's it for the night, time to vacate. But this couldn't have been further from the truth.

The coveys indigenous to these fields had been initially covered by a dusty powdering of snow, but the family gatherings were now shaking themselves of their icy shackles. This left them standing out well defined against the white ground. We couldn't believe our good fortune, and we reaped the benefits of accounting for over 90 birds that evening. On the way home the skies once again opened up, this time prolonged and it took us nearly an hour to travel the eight-mile journey home, our Hillman Avenger slipping and sliding on a ground its rear wheel drive wasn't designed to navigate.

The 70s and 80s were a time when profit hunters practiced their skills of taking partridges with a total disregard to capture or possible prosecution. Risks were constantly through the force that drove them, and at that time there was no greater taker of risks than myself. I ate from the plate of jeopardy and drank from a challis of excitement, which was only topped up by being out in the fields. One particular shall we say risky night, happened perchance when we once again left the cosiness of our front rooms in search of those little game birds, grey partridges.

Unfortunately on this evening in the field next to where we were to be functioning a combine harvester worked under lights in an attempt to reap the crop before the forecasted bad weather stole upon land awaiting the cold, wet visit. This however, never stopped our work, as the combine went away from us we scanned our field and shot partridge, when the machine turned and made its way back towards us, we squatted with our lights out. We knew the operator of the machine would never hear our shots over the top of the engine noise, and would be concentrating visually on the job in hand; we got away with it, and what an exciting night that was.

The best cartridges in those days for the task we found were Winchester two-and-a-half magnums. One in each chamber, and both barrels fired at the same time into the heart of the covey at a distance of around 10 yards ensured a great majority of the group were taken out. Then it was a job of picking up birds, most lying dead, others in the remaining throws of life bouncing like "jumping-jack" fireworks. When looking down the length of the fired barrels, it is easy to assess the success of the shots by the number of birds that are seen lifting. To ensure these birds were not lost, a couple of supposedly quieter inch cartridges were put into each gun chamber and the area searched with the lamp. Some of these birds would have been "pricked" so would have to be found as quickly as possible. Depending on the size of the covey, an average hit would account for between 8-12 birds, and in larger fields, there could be up to four separate family groups.

A decent evening's work for the profit hunters could be between 30-40 birds, and I've been party to obtaining many more in one night. These were at a time when the game dealers were paying on average £2.50 a young bird, and sometimes peaking over £3. Old birds were always lower, ranging from 50p to £1 each, but this differential between young and old birds was nothing else but a game dealer's scam. I cannot believe for one moment that anyone can distinguish a young partridge from an old bird once the two are skinned and lying on the table, and I doubt very much there exists a homosapien who possesses such a delicate pallet where they can detect old and young partridges once they have been cooked properly and served in a fine sauce.

Apart from game dealers we had a small amount of private buyers; one in particular was a Greek owner of a local fish and chip shop. This man regularly took large numbers of partridges at £2 per bird, irrelevant if they were young or old birds, with a fish supper for both of us for good measure.

During the height of our partridge hunting era I was also well into the throws of being a practicing taxidermist, this gave me another opportunity for reward from reaping large numbers of game birds such as partridge, by skilfully mounting them for any interested party to purchase or swap.

As well as selling these birds to game dealers or private buyers, many were used for the table; where the only drawback is their size. You may need more than a single bird to "fill yer pelt". When using partridge for my needs feathers were rarely plucked, I would rather skin the birds, use the carcase to eat, and mount the rest to sell on. All game birds are excellent birds to mount; their skin is thick compared to other species, and if an over-zealous finger does burst through, the skin can be successfully repaired with a needle and thread. As a mount partridges can look very attractive, set as a pair, one sitting and one standing, as depicted in the picture in one of my boyhood bibles, the *Observer's Book of Birds*. Individual birds that are too damaged for pristine mounting can be used to go under the grip of a raptor, mink or stoat.

Suddenly! Reality is restored, and unexpectedly my hand is touched by a wet nose, awakening me from my daydreaming by an old lurcher bitch that has remained faithful since the day my dextrous fingers broke her free from the fluid bag that she was delivered into the world in. This old girl has her dreams, and this has been evident many times when she lay twitching and whimpering on the carpet in front of our open fire. Yella too enjoys these reveries as she no longer possesses the speed to come to terms with a bolting rabbit, or the agility to match the dynamic twists and turns of a quick footed hare even if her keen eyes would have us believe different.

My eyes quickly search for the partridges which a few moments ago they focused on so absorbedly. There they are. Pecking and scratching, heads showing, and then disappearing. Oh what lovely birds they are, and what excellent hosts they have been this fine morning.

The sciatica pains are for the moment relieved, my old dog is impatient, and once again I leave a woman's grip totally satisfied. We set off from this special place with a rye smile, and then tip a wink towards Mother Nature and give a single wave of my trusty hazel stick towards a wonderful family who are the true owners of these fields and who deserve to be left in peace. I have had my dream, and once again the doors to the past are closed.

CHAPTER 8

The Strutting Country Gent

WHAT A beautiful specimen of a bird. So resplendent in its royal attire as he struts with pomp and ceremony akin to some important courtier of the bird world. An effervescent colouration that ceases to amaze whenever my eyes have the good fortune to examine. Who could have designed such a work of art? So why do we hunt this divine game bird for which there are not enough superlatives in the English language to describe? The pheasant.

The first introduced pheasants came from the Black Sea to Europe, and particularly to England in the 11th century, they have been interbred with the Chinese Common Pheasant (*Phasianus colchicus torquatus*) and the Japanese or Green Pheasant (*Phasianus versicolor*), giving the Ring-necked Pheasant (*Phasianus colchicus*).

Thinking back, it was the Albino Gypsy who educated me to taking pheasants and the fact that pheasants actually roosted away from the ground, amid the branches of bushes or trees, a piece of information I remember finding difficult to come to terms with. But they do, and although this ensures they sleep safely out of reach from nocturnal vulpine hunters it does lend them to be taken, sometimes in large quantities by that night-time skulker, the profit hunter.

Having listened to many grade Z poachers of how the best method of exercising their abilities of taking roosting pheasants is using a 4.10 shotgun, it always makes me duck and cringe as the twaddle excretes out their mouths in the form of verbal diarrhoea.

What the hell for? A good air rifle is easier to come by, it's quieter, there is no buck-shot to contend with when eating and this pneumatic weapon doesn't cost as much to run. A box of 500 Milbro-Caledonian .22 lead pellets cost us 1/6d and once the sights of the gun were zeroed in, the crimson faced head or the padded base of the neck of a cock pheasant were rarely missed.

The Albino in those early exploits used a catapult with three sixteenth square black elastic, and by god he could knock birds out of a tree with contemptuous ease. Never have I seen anyone draw back a catapult like him, the elastic almost reaching a yard in length before it was released. A short whistle for the bird to show its head then the smack if his aim was true or the dull thud of the lead ball, piece of iron ore or hand picked polished stone hitting heavy feathered protected breast flesh if his aim was off.

Pheasants hit in the head like this were going nowhere, I can assure you of that. Having read in airgun literature when comparing .177 and .22 of the shock factor, I have an awareness of the advantages and disadvantages of using either calibre. But a pheasant getting hit in the chest with such a missile propelled by a catapult must equate to us getting hit in the chest with a canon ball, so plenty of shock factor to contend with for the unsuspecting sleeping pheasant.

Taking roosting birds from the trees has always excited me with a passion, whether my hunting grounds were hawthorn hedgerows where a small number of birds were found sleeping, or deeper into the lion's den, where large numbers of disoriented birds from organised shoots picked some of the most impractical situates to kip. Wood pigeon can also be taken regularly using the same ploy, but for me they don't hold the same excitement as pheasants.

The first air rifle I ever used for this game in earnest was an old Webley mark 3, and what a fantastic little gun. These hard hitting airguns of their time were under-lever operated, well made and even boasted a walnut stock with a white disc bearing the maker's name set in this precious wood. Other guns such as Relam Tornadoes with their fancy shaped butts were tried, but their performance could never compare with the Webley, plus these Relams and other guns at that time, including the useful BSA Airsporter were all much larger, heavier and cumbersome. BSA did however make a most under-rated model that a few of my profit hunting friends used, the Mercury, but I always stuck to my Webley, until sheriff Patterson at Duns, looking over his square gold rimmed spectacles decided it was

Two male pheasants fighting.

time for the gun and myself to part company after over a 30-year or so love affair.

Later however, Webley brought out another compact air rifle, and although it could never compete with the incredible well made German air rifles that were taking over the British sporting rifle markets at that time, these English-made guns were very powerful, just on the legal limit of 12 foot-pounds, they were sturdy and more importantly, cheap. I bought mine when they first came out for £45 out of my mother's catalogue, paying a pound a week and I still have it to this day. It has killed many thousands of rabbits over the decades, mainly rabbits that were shot from the car window, or when a hunting chum and I walked and lamped rabbit-infested border lands. It has also accounted for vast numbers of pheasants, partridges, pigeons, hares and sea trout, yes fish, and I will furnish you dear reader into the ins and outs of this unusual past time in a later chapter.

In my younger days the sheer excitement of discovering the dark outline of a roosting pheasant led me to have a crack at it as quickly as possible, thinking all you had to do was to hit the bird and it was in the bag, but this couldn't be further from the truth, it's a game bird, not a starling.

A male pheasant.

The pheasant is a fairly large bird, it is quite heavily feathered, so the shock of a .22 calibre air rifle slug full in the chest or lower areas will do damage, but the bird can semi recover from the initial shock and will noisily fly away, just to die out of reach of the hunter, and maybe in a final resting that could alert a gamekeeper, farmer or shoot owner that the land was being poached. The ruckus noise they make will also put on guard any other roosting birds, and this will leave them nervous, sometimes lifting before the trigger is pulled again, or even just on hearing the approaching hunter's gentle footsteps treading on dry twig-covered forest floors. A bird that has not been scared will sit, sometimes while a number of unsuccessful attempts are made at hitting it.

The small .177 if used in most cases will penetrate the pheasants armour plating and hit vital organs, but again the bird can fly before it finally dies. So the witnessing of loosing a percentage of the birds I shot early on in my career taught me to always go for certain areas of the bird to ensure maximum effectiveness. This was to hit the bird in the head, or at the base of the neck, the crop area where the neck joins the body. Birds hit in any of these places will drop like stones from the tree, only if ever uttering the briefest of noises before bouncing on the woods' carpet with a dull thud. No matter how the bird was killed, it will bounce and flap violently and if left will leave tell tail signs of feathers all over the ground, so bids were always quickly picked up and put into Hessian carrying bags then the profit hunters clinically moved to the next roosting bird.

In my time both open sights and telescopic sights have been used. The layman may adopt the premise that scopes would be the best for the job. Well, they can be, but they need to be set up (as do open sights) but they are much easier knocked and therefore rendered less effective. I have used open sights probably 80% of the time when nocturnal hunting, and got to the point where very little was missed, so long as the light source you are using to illuminate the roosting bird is correctly positioned. Before each expedition sights of whatever type were zeroed in. For me this was done at a distance of between five and ten paces and the target was something like a bottle top, if the weather was accommodating the sights were adjusted outside in the back yard with my lurchers watching in wonderment, if it was raining the job was done indoors, with a copy of the wife's catalogue being used so pellets didn't ricochet all over the house.

In latter years I remember zeroing sights in on my 22 inch export model barrel Weirach HW35E (another tool confiscated by a Scottish Sheriff) and using a piece of hard wood as the target. The pellet hit the target, and in a nanosecond it came back toward me. When a pellet does this it is almost at the same trajectory as it went out, the pellet hit me smack in between the eyes, an inch either way and I would now be proof reading this manuscript with one eye. How lucky I was. Ever since this happened, I've always used something that the slug will easily sink into, or angle any piece of wood used.

Numbers wise the taking of pheasants was usually dictated by where the profit hunter was practicing his trade on the night. I had some really productive local places where a dozen or so birds could be accounted for on a regular basis to fill an order or use for my table, plus my dad always loved a pheasant dropped in for his tea. But, when big numbers were required the lion's den was visited, and any sort of tally could be taken on the night. Many times outings produced in excess of 200 pheasants. On one occasion the boot of our Vauxhall Viva was so full, birds were being squashed when the lid of the boot was being closed, and these vehicles had exceptionally large boot spaces, in fact poaching wagons of that era were classed as good or bad by the size of their boots. Vauxhall Viva's boots could hold five lurchers, Hillman Avengers took four.

The profit hunters' ideal time to acquire large hauls of pheasants was early on in the season, this is when the price offered by even the most crooked game dealers would be high. Once the initial numbers had been obtained in the markets however, the price would plummet akin to a falcon's dive. Over the years I had built up a good outlet for pheasants for when the market price went down this way, and right up to Christmas I could secure a price that made it worth while to go out and chance getting a few.

Head shots are required.

In all the years pheasants were taken at night, I have never entered the rickety all wire door of a keeper's pen. Yes, I've shot birds around the perimeters and sometimes even window shopped, but never stopped to buy from these pheasant supermarkets.

Knowing where the local shoots are is recognisance that all good pheasant poachers should know. Knowing where the pens are is also a must, these will hold the bulk of the birds, but once the shooting days have begun the birds will scatter, many may return to the sanctuary of their kindergarten or around its boundaries.

In hilly terrain however, once the birds have been driven to the guns from the higher plantations, pheasants will rarely fly or make their way back up steep hills, these birds will be easy picking for the profit hunter and trees and bushes in valleys and gorges after a shoot will house many birds. Gamekeepers will always have an increased edge on vigilance on the lead up to a shoot, and the profit hunter is aware of this, the actual evening of the shoot or a day or two after is when the best organised profit hunters will strike. Skilled men will always do their homework, but sometimes productive areas maybe found perchance.

On a cold November evening when checking a flowing burn for the migratory sea trout, we found a veritable plethora of roosting pheasants. The burn itself was set in a deep ravine surrounded by sloping Northumberland hills. When I got picked up at a pre-arranged meeting point, my colleague asked, "Anything in"?

"Not yet," I replied. "But we need to go back for the air rifle, the place is bloody heaving with pheasants."

We did go back that night and took over 90 birds. These were scattered birds, probably from a shoot that day, birds that hadn't yet established a regular roost, and sat in some of the most unlikely places imaginable, overhanging branches that we had to pass under, open branches of trees and bushes where as many as half a dozen birds were residing.

At one point I was working both light and gun, my co worker doing the picking up, the shooting was fast and birds were literally dropping all around my friend.

"For god's sake Dok," I remember him uttering. As I was deliberately taking out birds directly above him so as to fall on his head.

Apart from shooting pheasants after the blackbird had sung his final litany, pheasants were often taken again with the use of a good air rifle from the window of a vehicle. Driving along quiet country lanes with a few running dogs in the boot and one in the front of the car at our feet, plus an air rifle in the hands of the person riding shotgun, and the team was ready for bird or beast. Every gateway saw the vehicle slowing down, hawk like eyes gazing every inch of the field. Pheasants in many instances will squat, stand motionless or attempt to move off slowly, these will give a window of opportunity to quickly take aim, squeeze the trigger and shoot. Birds on fence posts or gates are sitters and rarely missed, but again, the aim must be quick.

Whether taking a few birds or a car boot-full of birds, nocturnal hunting of pheasants can be an exciting pastime. From my days as a young lad tagging behind the Albino gypsy with his catapult, to times when me and others of the same ilk donned our cloaks of invisibility and raided woods whose owners never knew we were coming. I have never tired of taking the opportunity of an outing in pursuit of this "strutting, country gent". The pheasant.

CHAPTER 9

Shooting Fish

THERE ARE various methods for illegally taking salmon and sea trout once the beckoning call of spawning beds where their lives begun entice them to return. Distant memories and imprinted instincts drive these fish to journey over a vast underwater universe from the Norwegian Sea and the waters off Southwest Greenland. The destination are the shingled playgrounds where, in their young "fry" state they joyfully swam and played chase me with hundreds of siblings amid pebbles, boulders and through fast flowing channels.

This goal is a most sacred quarter where again their fins will touch ground that once acted as their maternal protector. It has been many years for most fish since they tasted these sweet waters, and how they find their way back is still not fully understood, and remains one of nature's true phenomenas, an annual occurrence which the profit hunters constantly capitalise on.

In my days, any financial reward obtained from selling salmon or sea trout between the beginning of November and mid December was put into a jar. When the run of fish was over, the money was shared out, and this provided families with Christmas presents. With this bit of extra income kids had bikes, extra toys and a good Christmas, without it the festive season would have taken on a gloomier guise, and the main provider and master of the house would have felt a complete failure.

The tried and tested method of using gaff and torch has remained one of the profit hunters' favourites over many decades, in particular when the fish actually enter the shallow burns. When travelling up the roaring rivers from the sea, the same fish have already run the gauntlet of other enterprising poachers, whose preferred hunting method would be nets. These catching devices could either be long nets that stretched the entire width of the river, and also very effective short lengths which in many situations were more productive than their lengthier counterparts.

This part of my story is of a most unusual happening, late in the year when many of Mother Nature's creatures were well tucked up in their beds, and the countryside lay quite still with its eyelids tightly closed. The setting is a burn close to Alnwick in Northumberland, which at the backend of the year plays host to many migratory fish, mainly sea trout, as the river Aln which the burn flows into is not what could be classed as a fast flowing river, the type much preferred by salmon. The Aln's close neighbour the Coquet, and further up on the Scottish border the famous Tweed are the two closest salmon rivers, but the Aln does produce some cracking sea trout, and in large numbers.

The burn I speak of is relatively small in stature, but there is a saying among salmon poachers, "small burn big fish" and this was very true with this water. In places a man could straddle the burn, looking down on fish lying like logs, average fish size was 6lbs from this most productive place, and the largest single specimen I've seen taken was 13lbs.

We had many reconnaisance missions to this water checking if the fish were in. Other local burns had been teeming fish this season for many poaching teams from the townships of Ashington, Choppington and Bedlington, but this was a special burn for us, well worked each season for over 20 years and we knew every inch of it, where the best shingle beds were, which holes would house fish and where the fish could hide up under backsides to elude the night time skulker. This however, was a notorious late burn for fish. Its mouth was relatively small and during the spring and summer months it always built up a natural portcullis of weeds, and in the autumn months these weeds trapped many leaves, twigs and branches. The burn always required heavy prolonged rain to burst what would at times resemble a beaver's dam, and allow the waiting fish to enter.

It was now December 12 and getting close to Christmas, we had been doing fine; the jar was looking exceedingly well and the service of the Provident woman for an extra loan for Christmas was looking unlikely.

It had been raining for a day or two, but not what could be classed as heavy; a little rain had fallen on the morning of the day we decided to once again travel up to Alnwick, but this time not for fish. Around the vicinity of the burn there were various shoots, all of these syndicates had done some days, and there was a lot of scattered birds which roosted in the bushes and trees that aisled each side of the burn. We had quite a few orders for pheasants, and our own freezers required a top up, so this was an ideal opportunity to obtain a few birds while waiting for the rain we and the burn prayed for.

The poaching wagon owned by me at that time was a Daihatsu F50 jeep, a most useful tool that knocked the spots of any Landrover at that time in terms of reliability, off road ability, economy and comfort, its power unit was an amazing 2.5 diesel engine that wanted for nothing but fuel, oil and a drink of water. The vehicle's failing, it was a rust box. Possessing it however, allowed me to park on illicit trysts in some fantastic hiding places, sometimes two or three fields over from the main roads. It also didn't stand out like a sore thumb when spotted by the "feds" in the dead of night or early mornings, its CB antenna, bull bars and spot lights resembled it to a keeper's vehicle, and this saved our bacons on more than one occasion.

Now everyone who knows me is aware of my hatred of guns, mainly those weapons which kick when fired and leave black and blue bruises on the shoulders and cheeks of those of us who are shit frightened of them. A good air rifle however, is a favoured tool of my trade, and has been since the early days of BSA Airsporters and Mercury's Webley mark 3s and Relam Tornadoes. This night it was a weapon manufactured much later that travelled with us, my hard hitting Webley Vulcan .22, a lovely little gun which could be swung around easily in any car, and that had killed unbelievable amounts of game for us. We set off from Ashington around 1am, and reached our hunting ground by 1.30am.

This area is one of those places we would categorise as the "lions den" so extra special care and guile are always required on any visit, and this includes where to park a poacher's biggest give a way, the vehicle. Our favoured hideaway lay behind an old disused quarry, two fields from the road and approximately three miles from our burn. A different path was taken every time we frequented this stage, so as not to alert any Sherlock Holmes-type keeper finding a well worn track. No light was used on our trek down towards the burn, and speech was kept to a minimum. Our ears were alert to every noise as we walked quietly, and our eyes scanned for anything unusual; even in at times almost complete darkness. It's astonishing what can be detected at night as a possible alert. A linnet breaking from a roosting place in dense gorse, it could have been a marauding fox or a searching stoat or weasel that startled this little musical finch from his slumber, but for us it could also be a crouching keeper or bailiff. Do we take a chance, or make a hasty retreat? Even our noses at times can act as early warning devices. Being a non-smoker and non-drinker, my olfactory powers are finely honed to these odours. Several times my nasal senses have met with either of these drifting in the darkness. Was it another poaching team? Was it a keeper or farm hand sitting in a hedge back on poacher patrol? I don't know, we never stopped long enough to find out.

Treading secretively we eventually arrived at the first line of swaying trees where in the past we had witnessed pheasants roosting. The dark shapes of these birds silhouetted against the dark indigo sky. We began, taking the birds in the lower branches. My gun was raised toward the roosting bird, and I indicated to my companion I was ready. The light went on, from behind my right shoulder towards the bird. As quick as a kingfisher the sight of the gun zeroed in on the red face of the pheasant, the trigger was squeezed, the gun fired and a noise like the pellet striking a rock rang out. My friend immediately switched off the beam of light, and the bird fell out of the tree hitting the ground with a hollow thud. Our eyes were fully accustomed to the darkness, and the light wasn't required as we picked up the flapping bird and put it quickly into a Hessian bag to lesson the chance of feathers being dispersed all over the damp ground. Within a few seconds the flapping stopped completely indicating this beautiful bird's life had ebbed, the

Fresh run salmon.

end of strutting quiet country lanes for such a resplendent game bird. Time to move on and go for the next, we have an order to fill.

Over a dozen plump birds had been taken when we approached a small gap in the trees, a space used by the farmer as a crossing where the large wheels of his tractor would easily negotiate such a watery crossing. Suddenly from the darkness came the sound of heavy splashing. In the blink of an eye my chum and I were competing in the 100 metre hurdles back towards safety, there had been no time to think, it was one of those times when the natural defences of the body cries fight or flight.

Now I've been chased across fields before so I know what it's like. For some reason it's always been accompanied by bouts of shouting.

"Come back here", "Stop" and other such phrases that a profit hunter would take no notice of.

There was no shouting, no sense of being watched or pursued and none of the gut feelings you have when you become the chased. My friend must have sensed this too, as we both slowed down at the same time and looked back into the eerie darkness.

"What do you think Dok," asked my friend.

"Dunno, but its definitely not keepers, they would have been on us by now, and well organised bailiffs would be surrounding us like Indians at Custer's last stand."

We peered silently, our throats burning, our hearts pounding and our breathing heavy.

"Could have been a deer crossing," I said uncertainly.

A few more minutes and our brave heads came back on.

After a time we decided to cautiously go back, setting off back down the embankment, warily treading through the damp grass, out heads cocked to one side in an attempt to detect any unwelcome noise.

As we neared the trees once again we heard the noise of splashing, this time we were mentally ready, and we stood our ground and listened.

"Well, it's not a deer," I said with a degree of irony.

Into the tree line we walked, the water of the burn could be seen twinkling even in this dark setting. We approached the water's edge, and shone the light into the shallow water. What a sight, there were fish lying everywhere. Six, seven, eight, nine. Loads of fish, a light, but no bloody gaff. The gaff end was always in the jeep, hidden in the material of the roof cloth, where the roof met the jeep's side panels. The shaft of the gaff just lay in the back of the jeep; it was just another

Legally taken salmon.

stick lying among others cut to be used in my making of walking sticks. The jeep however, was over three miles away.

After a time of watching these lovely creatures gently holding their positions in the flowing water with slow continuous gentle waves of their tails, we decided to have a go at shooting them with the air rifle.

The barrel of the loaded gun was slowly put into the water till it almost touched the top of the head of one of the fish, closer and closer till the tip was about a quarter of an inch from our prey. I pulled the trigger and the stunned fish rolled over and floated to the surface without so much of a flap of a fin. Both my friend and I looked at each other in total amazement. Then a short delay before the fish was lifted lifeless from the ice cold water, while at the same time fumbling cold fingers inserted another slug into the breach of the cocked gun. Another shot and another fish, this was all so, so easy. Within a few minutes all nine sea trout had been taken from this stretch.

With our spoils lying in a regimental straight line on the grassy bank side, it was now decision time. Do we settle for the swag of pheasants and fish, or do we go for more.

We are profit hunters, not one for the pot men. We tramped back to the vehicle to get the gaff. As this point on the burn was a fair way from the mouth, we believed that if the fish were here, there would be plenty of other opportunities for fish on the other stretches known to us.

After our mammoth trek and now armed with our trusted gaff we did the burn from a short distance from the mouth to where we shot our first fish, this gave us 46 fish in total, plus the pheasants we began the night with. The next night we returned and took another 40 fish and the following night a further 18.

Over the three nights the total number may represent a very good haul, but far from being our best. It does however, remain in our minds, not just for the tally, but for the unusual way in which the first nine fish were taken. With the good old Webley Vulcan .22 calibre air rifle, shooting fish!!!

CHAPTER 10

A Fisherman
Not an Angler

FISHING has always consumed some part of my waking life over the years. As a youngster so much excitement and enjoyment was obtained whether fishing with green heart rod and Scarbourough reel in the cold steel grey north sea, using a hand line off a pier, staiths and beach or that magic feeling the whippiness of split cane fishing in streams and river while listening to the joyful music these fast flowing waters sang. I may speak as an angler, but an angler I am not; I am a fisherman, and a profit hunting fisherman to boot.

Even later in life I profit from the enjoyment of a day's fishing, these outings providing me solace from the pressures of work and everyday life, a speed of society that at times I find difficult to come to terms, or keep up with. Although I do enjoy these outings, I am still first and foremost a numbers man, and considerably more pleasure comes from having caught 20 fish than from catching one. In my fishing box I cannot resist taking a jar of my mate Spike's "taffy" to let my worms play games of chase me through before I attach them to my hook. Fishing for monetary profit came later in my life and the important factor at this time of my evolution was "how many have you got" not "how did you catch them". But the reveries from fishing expeditions from my youth are just as strong as those from my latter profit hunting years, and I always enjoy pondering over them in times of quiet gladness.

As the dog and I left the main road and sauntered down the winding track past Joe Binney's farm, I said to him, "Duke I'm really looking forward to this expedition, I think we are going to have a good day's fishing." The dog showed his understanding and appreciation of my happiness by rubbing against my leg, his tail wagging and then he excitedly darted off into the untidy undergrowth on the scent of a rabbit that had passed earlier. What a wonderful time of my life I have the privilege of looking back on.

I sat on the high grassy bank side above the river Blyth, the seat was damp, but to me this resting place was a throne and for a brief moment in time I was a King. Sovereign of a countryside that smiled so endearingly. As acting monarch all the treasures are strategically arranged around me. To the right fields of nebulous gold, corn that swayed as if dancing to the whispering melody of the wind. To my left, a mantle of lush pasture so green and well washed the finest emeralds that mother earth spawned would have been jealous of its patina, a grassland that sociably invites partridge to rummage and skylark to nest. Below me the lapping water's edge shimmers with silver and a myriad of sparkling gems as the sun's rays play upon it, what riches this boy-king possesses.

This part of my river is tidal, and the water was about another two hours from being at its highest point. Two hours at each side of both high tide and low tide are the most productive times to fish this stretch for eels, those long and very slippery creatures.

The author's son with a trout.

I baited the treble hook with a juicy earthworm, recently dug from the front garden of my parent's home; my rod must have sensed we were going to be successful and this seemed to magnify its whippiness for my first cast of the day. The lead sinker dived headlong into mysterious waters with a resounding plop, and the slack line was reeled in, not so much as to get a "fast had" or in angling terms, getting snagged on the many boulders and rocks that littered the river's

The little grebe, a fisherman.

black mud covered floor. The rod was laid on a spiny clump of grass, a most perfect natural rod stand, now it was a game of patience, a virtue which I have always possessed in great abundance.

Searchingly my fingers probed through the grass and sphagnum moss into the soil, feeling for nuggets of iron ore to throw into the murky waters. This area was once the heart of a thriving iron industry, and many natural deposits still lay waiting to be found, but instead of meeting their fate in the smelter they would be slung out of catapults by young boys on their explorations. I scanned the surroundings with eyes so alert, so keen they missed nothing that flew, ran or crawled.

Duke, my trusted canine companion and at times confidant sat close. The dog's ears were pricked and alert like those of Anubis guardian of the Egyptian god's underworld, his lustrous eyes watched every missile launched, and with every rippling splash Duke twitched, cocking his head to one side as if questioning should he fetch it or not.

From the corner of my eyes I spotted the dog's inquisitiveness.

"Don't even think about it my hairy friend."

The dog sensed my awareness, and with its wet tongue proceeded to wash his young master's face. Spitting, and at the same time shoving the dog away with my forearm I laughingly ordered, "Duke stop it."

The dog saw this as a game, and continually fought for my attention. We rolled and tumbled in the long grass, the dog's powerful jaws mouthing over my forearm, his teeth digging softly into my skin but never penetrating or causing me harm, what a friendship betwixt this boy and dog.

Our antics were disturbed as my eyes detected movement on the tip of my fishing rod. Slowly lifting the rod I waited till I could feel the rapid pulling of something taking the bait. Then I struck hard as if it were a fine trout that had risen and taken a floating nymph on the end of my line, unnecessary of course, as with a trebler in its mouth a slippery eel will rarely escape. The duel between the eel and myself commenced, a short contest, as bringing in even the largest eel is akin to pulling in a weight, yes you can feel its wriggling telegraphed up the entire length of the line and up through the rod, but it lacks the power diving and fight of a fit sea trout or salmon.

On to the bank came the eel with a final flick of the rod, and Duke dived onto the wriggling snake-like creature, pawing it, and grabbing at it with flashing ivory teeth, no friendly biting with this guy. Dropping the rod and calling Duke to one side, I held the eel in my hand, and immediately it wrapped itself around my wrist and forearm. I was fighting to remove the hook from its pointed mouth, my fingers continually being pushed aside by the coils of its slimy, smooth body. It was no good so I dropped my catch and quickly found a stout piece of branch and whacked the eel, aiming for its head, but striking it across its back as it threshed, not enough to stop it but enough to slow it down. My next shot had truer aim, and the branch struck just behind the creatures head, the contest was over. Now a time for an anatomical examination, a Darwin-like going over of every inch of my river Blyth eel. It's amazing how much fascination a dead creature's body holds for the young enquiring mind of a country boy, armed with a stick to overturn and prod and dextrous finger to manipulate into various shapes and poses. Ah, sheer profit hunting bliss.

Travelling almost 50 years along thrilling journeys armed with mackerel flies, shore lines and west winders I eventually came to a time in every profit hunter's life where opportunities are seized to capitalise on, to secure both excitement and pocket money. A knew apprenticeship was now taking place, guided by mentors such as my old friend Billy Wright (Spike) and his partner in crime Carlton, or Lord Ford as those in the court of fish poaching called him. Both these guys were experts in the taking of fish, but they were both primarily

A fisherman, the osprey.

net men, where, although I did participate on cold outings with both nets that stretched across a river and short lengths to fish eddy's close to the river banks, it was using gaff and torch that excited me more. But, akin to any grade A student, I listened, and learnt, obtaining a priceless education that would ensure that I and any team would take numbers, but also to be safe from well organised bailiffs. Although we never got captured, I'm not saying for one moment we didn't have any close encounters, as with the volume of times we hunted, it would be folly to believe we were never detected.

There are many burns that can be successfully gaffed in the area of Northumberland where I live, these could never be covered by bailliffs ensuring these networks of waters were protected fully from poaching gangs. Bailiffs rely not only on their nightly patrols, but also from what we call "bailliff's narks", individuals such as keepers, farmers, landowners and legal fishermen, who would inform them of any "goings on" in the area. Once alerted, river bailiffs watch and wait, finding out where the activity is happening, how the poachers are getting on and off the burn, any parking places that are being used. This is the reconnaisance they require to eventually spring their trap. Bailiffs may let the poacher have some successful nights while they

A fisherman, a northern gannet.

are information gathering, lulling the hunting team into a false sense of security, a ploy that works well in apprehending those who are not au fait with their methods. Keeper or farmer activity is more rush headlong in for the chase, where bailiff action is more of a military manoeuvre, which reminds me!

One burn we visited regularly was close to the Otterburn army training camp in north Northumberland, close to the Carter Bar. This was a lovely crystal clear burn coming from its source in the hills and wending its way snake-like to the river Rede which meant any fish were originally Tyne fish. These waters possess unbelievable clarity and the wild brown trout the Rede contains possess a most beautifully yellow under belly. The waters are fast flowing, ensuring the perfect environment for a large number of salmon rather than sea trout.

This burn yielded many good hauls, and apart from our first ever outing on it, provided us with no major scares. We did however, have a game plan that seemed to work well before any gaffing took place, by travelling across fields to the point where when gaffing, would be our ending place, a point where the burn came out of woods and travelled with no cover through exposed hills and fields. We would then follow the burn making sure that no one was about, or any vehicles parked "clocking" the burn. We would then walk the burn back towards the mouth, and gaff fish when found. This goes against the text book ideal of walking up stream gaffing as you go. But, all burns are individual, and it worked for this stretch of salmon-infested water.

Over the years nightly numbers of fish could amount up to 40, which is a lot of mass to be carried. The average size of these good quality fish could be up to eight pounds, so quite a lot for two men to carry almost five miles over such hostile terrain to the pick up point.

One night, during our preliminary checking out the burn, there was something wrong, a feeling I just couldn't put my finger on, but since that day a feeling that my friend said he also had that evening. Silently we walked over damp sodden grass and fir needles, our eyes scanning, straining in the dark as at no point were our lamps illuminated. Then a feeling that someone is close, very close.

"I think we should abort the mission," I whispered to my chum.

Just as the words left my lips, from all sides men rushed out from the trees, lamps shone at us, the whole place alive with lights, noise and hostile activity. That's us knackered I thought to myself, bailiffs. I was unceremoniously pushed to the ground, my hands tied behind my back with a nylon cable tying device. Hold on, these are going a

bit too far. I could only manage to see a boot in front of me, the size
and condition of which didn't suggest the vendor was an aficionado of
church outings or ballroom dancing. Suddenly I was picked up off the
ground, spitting moss and soil from lips that had been shoved into the
damp ground. Normal sight restored, I was greeted by a gang of men
the size and likes which I had only ever witnessed before outside the
doors of the Domino night club at Bedlington Station in the 1960s.
These were army men, not sure if SAS, but definitely some elite
fighting force on manoeuvres from the camp.

"What the hell you doing here," asked a camouflaged, painted face
fire spitting man mountain. A morbid sense of curiosity fought to
replace my terror, as I summoned up the last vestige of courage to
answer such angry demanding questioning.

"Fishing," I nervously replied. I was lowered from his grasp and
oh how good it felt to have my feet back on ground that they were
designed to walk on rather than paddling like a duck in mid air.
Walking at this point, indeed running like hell seemed to be an idea,
but maybe not a good idea.

The whole situation seemed to mellow, my friend was now next
to me and we co-explained the technical workings of gaffing fish, in
fact when our bonds were cut, our tears wiped and soiled underpants
changed, and a cigarette offered to calm our nerves it became quite a
cosy little setting, reminiscent of men sitting around the camp fires in
the film Blazing Saddles. We even caught a fish for them to show off
our hunting prowess.

After some good crack, the main man advised us that they always
did maneuvers on Thursday nights, and regularly in this location, and
that we should avoid this burn at least on these nights. We did miss
out this burn on Thursday evenings, and we were never bothered by
the army again, whether or not they were there on other evenings
when we fished observing us we will never know.

The burn however, was a lucrative place and its appeal always
won the scuffle when deciding to maybe do lesser safer waters with
less fish. Minor adjustments would need to be made, apart from the
avoidance of certain nights, if we were to continue being successful
there. So we became well armed with the ordinance survey map for
the area showing every track running through the forest, and a key
obtained from a woodsman that fitted every forestry commission lock.
These tools opened the windows of opportunities to drive to a good
vantage point through the trees virtually undetected.

Driving on the main highway to the edge of the forest, and within half a mile there was a single bar gate. We opened the lock using the acquired key, and drove in locking the gate behind us. We then drove up the ride with only the sky's feint light to guide us till we came to a left turn, the vehicle which we had actually borrowed from work was then parked and we covered the rear lights with black plastic bin liners. Side lights on we followed our map to our destination where we made ready and did the business. This was profit hunting organization at its best.

One evening the lock had been changed, a bright new device hung on the gate to stop intruders. This was the first warning sign, which immediately put us into wary mode. The key still fit the new lock, so we cagily entered our secret domain, following the same pattern as usual, trying to block out the new lock from our minds after thinking of realistic reasons why it should have been changed.

Around the first corner while fitting the covers to the giveaway red tail and stop lights, we heard a vehicle engine. We went to the ride and looking down could see a vehicle was parked at the gate. We watched as someone got out and examined the gate, got back in the car and left, turning right towards the Scottish border. My heart was pounding, I know my friend's was too as I could literally hear it through his worn Barbour jacket.

Kingfishers.

A legally caught trout.

"What we going to do Dok," he asked.

"Well, I know what we are not going to do, and that's go fishing tonight," I replied.

We turned the vehicle and made toward the gate, frightened in case the same vehicle pulled back in. The lock was opened by dexterous nervous fingers and we got out, replacing the lock.

"I'm going right," I said to my mate. The expression on his face suggested he wasn't up for it. I just wanted to see if there was any activity further down the road, a parking place known to us where bailiffs could park. As we passed, a number of Vauxhall Astramax vans were assembled, yip, we had visitors of the bailiff kind. We just passed and not having anywhere we could turn, continued along the road, however one van pulled out and began to follow us. We kept on going; still the van was on our tail. It wasn't till after we crossed the border into Scotland that the van stopped, we continued and went home to civilization and reality via the towns of Kelso and Wooler.

This episode might sway people into thinking that we never did that burn again, but we did. These things will happen from time to time; they make us more vigilant, more aware and ensure we create new adaptations to strengthen routines. Animals that are creatures of habit or routines are more likely to be caught than those that chop and change. The profit hunter's ethos is to realize this, and to make sure that routines and patterns are not made for others to capitalize on.

CHAPTER 11

The Big Fellas

E VEN AS MY life winds down, I cannot allow over 50 years' experience in the local fields of my native Northumberland go to waste. Building up intimate relationships with bird and beast, and developing an affinity with wildlife has taken forever to forge. Knowing my quarry has always been a fundamental prerequisite of being a profit hunter. Over the last decade however, many adaptations have had to be made. The main tool of my trade may now be my camera and my expert prowess in the field is now exercised by getting into position to photograph what would have been potential quarry in the past, and profit now comes in a much different form. I have previously mentioned that my main quarry species may have been the humble rabbit, but there was a time in my evolution when I was literally obsessed with another of our endemic game species, the roe deer.

The wild lands of Northumberland have always housed a great wealth of roe, and the profit hunter never needed to travel to far off places to enjoy their sport, and I agree with the man who wrote, "The eyes of a fool are in the ends of the earth". Virtually on my doorstep these lovely creatures are found, and, by the aspiring deer hunter, taken using a myriad of methods. On glib wasteland previously owned by the National Coal Board I have the good fortune of walking and in less than a mile can regularly observe roe deer. In the past travelling less than five miles took me into some of the most productive Shangri-La's for obtaining deer with dogs.

Imprinted in my mind are exhilarating expeditions into Mother Nature's back gardens in pursuit of roe, and I can still remember when, after exhaustive endeavours with a lurcher bitch that many believed to be too small for the purpose, her first deer was taken.

It was a raw October morning when my poaching partner and I drove through the Blagdon estates in Northumberland owned by Lord Ridley in a hand-painted green Hillman Avenger. Now having previously met the landowner, we were not exactly drinking chums, remembering the time when he pulled up on horseback one morning at a gateway I was parked in watching the activities of the local hunt.

"The dogs went that way," I excitedly said to him pointing in the general direction the pack of hounds eagerly travelled in pursuit of their exhausted prey.

A roe buck.

Red deer stags in Scotland.

"Hounds bastard," he replied, and rode off. It seems that some people may have been born into privilege, but obviously may have been bypassed in being taught basic politeness. My dextrous fingers scratched the ground and picked up a rounded pebble and I angrily threw it with the power of an American baseball pitcher, but the old man's speed on his hunter cross was such that he was out of my range.

We poached Blagdon estates showing no remorse for decades, taking many hundreds of deer and hare, we also shot roosting pheasants from trees and partridges from car windows during the daylight hours and in tilled fields at night. Trout-filled ponds were almost emptied and burns "sheckle netted" for the brownies that lived there. What a most productive area this was, for the offended profit hunters.

The narrow road we travelled winded down towards a hump-backed bridge. Over the steep rise the old Hillman chugged and "pinked". At the other side, standing momentarily staring right at us was a female roe deer. In a split second she turned and began to flee up the road, her white rump bouncing as she ran.

Lurchers in the boot of the Hillman.

I stood on the brake pedal and the car came to an abrupt stop, chippings from the road peppering the underside of the vehicle. An excited panic ensued as we opened the car doors and literally fell out, followed by two lurcher dogs diving over the top of us fired by excitement of their maiden chase of this much larger adversary than what they were used to. The dogs took off at speed, their nails noisily scratching at the tarmac for grip as they accelerated.

Even on this most hostile running stage the dogs quickly caught up with the fleeing deer. The deer struggled to find an escape route along a road that was aisled with thick hedges. There was a gateway further up the lane, but she wasn't to know this, and she turned and made her way back towards the untidily parked car and excited observers, the dogs unable to show off their usual turning abilities jinked cautiously and once again were quickly on the back of her.

At this point I was contemplating a possible Jackie Pallo drop kick, but in a split second my black bitch Bes overtook the much larger lurcher Dixy and struck at the deer, spinning it and causing the creature to crash into the long grass that shared the verge with tangled brambles, dock and meadowsweet. Again Bes was first in and began a frenzied attack on the screaming, threshing beast. Dixy followed, and then me to dispatch what was the first deer taken by one of my dogs.

The blue touch paper was now lit, rocketing me into the world of deer poaching, an activity that brings its rewards, but also many possible downfalls. Being stopped by keen traffic police in the early hours of the morning and possessing a boot full of rabbits is one thing, but possessing a roe deer carcass, well, no policeman in this situation will turn a blind eye I can assure you of that.

One lucky escape we had was when we travelled back from Wooler with a deer in the boot of the car. We had also put the dogs in the boot with the carcase, so they would be undetected if we passed any police vehicles. Going up the bank at Weldon Bridge a traffic police vehicle sat parked up, its single occupant questioning every car that travelled past. Instantly its lights went on and came after us.

After a mile or so we were pulled over, this was it I thought to myself, at least in jail we were guaranteed our Sunday dinners.

"Where you been lads," the officer asked.

Female deer.

Red deer stag.

"Looking for permission," I replied. Well you have to tell them something, you can't just say we've been poaching and there's a deer in the back.

"Got anything you shouldn't have in the boot?"

"Just dogs," I answered.

"Dogs in the boot," he said questionly. "Lets have a look."

Slowly I began to raise the boot lid, three heads popped out, pushing to get out.

"That's enough," the copper said. "Just close the boot, don't let them loose on the main road." We got away with it that night, and this remains one of the closest close shaves I've ever experienced .

Taking deer with dogs stayed a large part of my hunting life for many years, and at one point we were taking in excess of a 100 roe a year with our dogs, with night time vigils pre-planned for taking deer only, and on some of these evenings accounting for up to five beasts. At this time it was not actually an offence, in England, to take deer with dogs, it was in Scotland, I was told. Gradually however, the excitement and any early romanticism abated, mounted heads and antlers no longer adorned the walls of my home and kennel blocks and it became my hunting premise that if I saw a deer in the lamp's searching beam it would be raced, but going out specifically for deer became a thing of my past. I've done it and worn many, many tee-shirts. Roe deer with dogs, well with my dogs I found them easy, they are just big daft hares, a mixture of intelligence, speed, stamina but at times, stupidity. There are however, as with hares, some that on the day take off and run with a determination that practically no running dog will match.

CHAPTER 12

The Deer Slayer

A SUCCESSFUL night on the lamp always stirs an excitement that flows through my very soul, exhilaration that makes it nigh impossible for me to get to sleep after the event. Returning home, feeding and bedding down my dogs, then sitting slurping a cup of weak, milky tea and demolishing a packet of custard creams as I write up the evening's events in my little black diary, are a "must be done" as part of my winding down process.

After an evening where my dog did amazingly on a hare that should never have been caught I have relived every jink and every turn as the creature did its best to shake off a dog that was almost its shadow in its last few moments on this earth. Even in sleep thoughts are rekindled and once again in my dreams I stealthily tread damp fields of my beautiful Northumberland with two keen dogs by my side.

Over the years many lurchers have took residence in my well constructed draft-free kennels, and there was not one of them that couldn't take a roe deer. My best all-round lurcher, Bes, would take roe deer easily. My best rabbiting bitch was Bes's granddaughter Yella and she also took out the occasional roe but my best deer dog ever was Kit.

Kit was 24 inches at the shoulder, a black broken-coated black bitch out of Bes and Billy Mercels Paddy dog. What a paring that was, a mating that took three years in the planning and 20 minutes in conception. The litter also produced a very useful dog called Cap, who was the sire of Yella. On rabbits Kit could be hitty-missy, the most

Kit the deer slayer.

rabbits in one night she accounted for was 32, but rabbit didn't excite this bitch in the way they did her illustrious hunting relatives. She would often go "stale" on them, choosing to not even run them, at other times she would run with the determination of a Sherman tank, only to drop the rabbit alive a few yards from me, and when the creature ran away, Kit wouldn't run it a second time. What a headache this bitch was for me at times, and blame was focussed on the small piece of fickle collie blood that ran through her veins for this fault.

It was on one of those "bad head nights" when the antidote was discovered. Kit had caught around half a dozen rabbits when she began what we will call her negative side. Having Yella out on the same night on the double slip however meant a good haul remained almost a guarantee.

At this point in her upbringing Kit would still be classed as a sapling to many others. I allow every dog I have ever possessed to have a maximum of three faults, but as a dogman I don't afford the same luxury, as I have so many shortcomings it would be impossible to list them all, but one of these imperfections has always been I didn't let my dogs have a childhood, the target of every pup I entered was 100 rabbits before they reached a year old. Kit was 14 months old now and had well over 300 rabbits in the book, but as yet no hares.

In the beam of light from my Lucas square eight a hare was running broad side on from us, both dogs immediately reared up on to their hind legs pulling in the direction of the supercharged beast. My hand searched for the quick release, but not on Yella's collar, Kit was mistakenly slipped.

After the hare she ran like a dog possessed. The hare jinked and ran for all its worth and at one point the squeals of an animal who was realising there was nothing it could do to shake off its pursuer rang out in the lit up eerie darkness. A couple more futile attempts to escape before Kit's frothing jaws clamped like a vice across its back.

No half-heartedness with this quarry, the creature was dead in seconds and Kit carried her spoils back and dropped the limp creature at my feet. Kit's first hare yes, but this was to have many other hidden benefits for my dog. On the rabbits she chased for the remainder of the evening she showed no mercy. She missed very little and my old girl Yella was left almost a redundant spectator as my concentration focussed almost totally on Kit.

This almost performance enhancing drug lasted a few more nights out, before Kit slipped back into the abyss of annoyance. On future excursions whenever Kit got a bit stale, my profit hunting partner would say, "She needs another hare Dok!"

This went on until Kit was almost two years of age, then the anti was upped a bit, when on a windy night north of the Scottish border near Abbey St Bathams Kit accounted for her first roe. Until our dogs actually race something as big as a deer, or a creature that bites back, we can never be fully sure of any hunting outcomes on these diverse forms of prey.

On lamping trips to Caledonia we usually had a plan. We knew really good ground near Duns where deer could be worked in such a way that almost ensured regular success. The land consisted of a large field that stretched its green fingers from the road towards a large plantation, the grassland possessed many dips and hollows where deer would feed out on even the most windy of nights and also when the moon cast its silvery light upon the sleeping land. The concaves gave the feeding deer shelter, while the wind blew above them towards their home of violently swaying fir trees in the distance.

Our plan at this stage was one of us on each flank, and to get into position at least three quarters of the way to the woods. Only then would a light be switched on. The beam of light would scan like a light house. If the green/blue eyes of a deer was spotted a quick flash

towards each other and the chase proper was on. Now coursing deer in the dark in this way will require some discipline, otherwise it becomes a free for all with sword fencing lights swishing to and fro with no end product other than tired dogs and awoken land. A dog on the back of a deer over a 100 yards away on the other side of the field doesn't require another dog to be slipped at this point. A dog taking the deer across the field towards the other hunter however, well that's another story. We want this chase to be a short story, not War and Peace. We were so successful with our plan of attack in this environment that when we worked the setting we rarely failed in catching at least one roe deer.

This was just the initial part of our three part Caledonian hunting plan. The second part was to lamp the arses off our dogs on rabbits and anything else runable that came into our beams of light. The third and final phase of our night time vigil saw us parking up in some shadowy retreat till breaking light, and race a few hares or possibly a deer on country roads during the long journey south.

It was on the afore mentioned Scottish setting where Kit caught her first deer, using the ploy previously mentioned, after some good running by Billy's Paddy dog. Kit nailed the beast when my lamp startled the running creature into resembling Bambi on the ice as it came towards me. They all count.

This was Kit's first deer, and the event was similar to the frenzied attack of a shoal of piranha, the violent brutality of the Psycho shower scene. Slowly came the realisation that this was no ordinary deer dog I had in my possession, and deer took over from hares as the remedy to any bug of staleness that occasionally crept into Kit's performances on bunnies.

Kit's prowess on creatures bigger than herself grew and grew with every season. Over the decades I have observed some very good deer dogs, some that caught these larger adversaries with a contemptuous ease. But Kit not only caught deer, she killed them with contemptuous ease.

One evening, and again over the border Kit and Paddy were slipped on to two feeding roe, each dog taking a separate deer. Paddy pulled his down quite quickly, but Kit's ran her out of my beam. In the lengthy time it took us to sort out Paddy's kill, Kit was nowhere to be seen. She had run her prey towards a plantation, so I was expecting

Opposite: *The profit hunters' dogs, Kit, Bes, Paddy and Rush.*

her to be showing any second, as not many roe deer are taken once they have made it to the sanctuary of woods they see as their homes.

We decided to put our deer next to the fence line and go looking for Kit.

We were almost at the plantation when my searching spotlight spotted the silhouette of Kit, she was standing over the deer a few yards from the fence line, and the creature was stone dead. Had it been known what the internal damage was I wouldn't have ran the 170-mile gauntlet taking the beast home, the carcase would have been left for fox and buzzards. On skinning this deer never have I witnessed so much damage, almost every inch of the meat was bruised, the front legs were completely pulled from their sockets, the rib cage was smashed as if it had been hit by a two-ton Landrover, and teeth holes peppered every bit of the saddle as if it had been taken out with triple As. Only about a quarter of the carcass was salvaged for the table, and it only got consumed as I don't mind bruised meat, it helps make a lovely gravy, but it would never have sold. This was the trait, of Kit the deer slayer, one of the fastest, tightest turning lurchers I've ever seen, a loveable bitch that killed more deer in her working career than she did hares, before she was stolen by individuals from Ashington in 1990.

CHAPTER 13

The Ultimate Quarry

O F ALL THE endemic creatures to Great Britain that I have hunted, none holds as much fondness, nay, admiration than our wonderful brown hare. My respect of this creature commands a passion to the point where after a long successful race with one of my dogs I would sit for ages with this beauty at my feet, staring at it in wonderment, examining the creature with gentle, probing fingers. In the past I have persecuted the beast, but hunting the hare at one time in my life seemed right. Oh how time changes us, age has mellowed me, as nowadays my mind would never possess thoughts of killing such a captivating mammal, but the memories and experiences of taking this creature, using a myriad of hunting methods, I am for the time willing to share.

Hares and their relatives the rabbits comprise the zoological order Lagomorpha. Modern biochemical evidence has suggested these lagomorphs have been a distinct lineage for around 90 million years. Since the dinosaurs became extinct around 65 million BP (years before present) experts say that it is possible that hare-like creatures were scurrying about the feet of the giant reptiles for around 25 million years.

Until relatively recently lagomorphs were confused with rodents. Lagomorphs are unique in having a small pair of secondary incisor teeth in the upper jaw, just behind the main pair. These are never present in rodents and clearly distinguish the two animal groups.

Bes and Fly with hares.

The brown hare is thought to have evolved in continental Europe, but probably did not move northwards before Britain was cut off from the mainland by the formation of the English Channel. If this was so, then the mountain hare is our only native hare species. The brown hare was possibly introduced by the Romans or by an even earlier civilisation.

In my native Northumberland the hare has always been found in good numbers. North Northumberland and the Scottish borders are bastions for the brown hare, and geographical locations where almost all of my hare hunting took place. Places on the Scottish borders such as Mindrum, Pressen and Carem where I had the good fortune to legally hunt hares using fit lurchers with respected people such as the Hon PWJ Fairfax, Basil Smalley and Ted Walsh, all gentlement highlighted in Ted Walsh's book, *Lurchers and Longdogs*. There are also many other areas where I hunted these creatures illicitly using air rifle, dogs, gatenets and longnet.

Before witnessing the hunting prowess of the dogs belonging to the Albino gypsy, it was my father's whippets used in the task of attempting to secure a strong local hare. In this era whippets were not the large whippets we witness today, my dad's dogs weighed approximately 14lb, and in some cases it took both the dogs he had to catch and hold a full grown hare. In these days it was only the occasional hare that was taken.

Then came lamping, and lurchers replaced the diminutive whippet for me and many others, mainly for catching larger numbers of rabbits, but hare also became a more frequent quarry taken by our dogs in numbers never seen before.

I have never been one of those hunters who bemoan hare killing with dogs on the lamp, I've done it, and I've enjoyed every minute of it, and if I still kept running dogs today, I would still be doing it. I've seen 20 plus hares killed by a team of well groomed lurchermen in one night's work, men organised, working as a team over the undulating contours of the land and allowing dogs to take their turn to share the workload over a night's graft. I have also witnessed hares being raced on the lamp that no lurcher would have ever caught. The bemoaners of lamping hares suggest that this activity is done by those whose dogs could take a hare in the daylight hours, what a load of piffle and bilge. Our dogs took good numbers of hares on the lamp, but also in the daylight, this is the advantage of having good dogs as opposed to average dogs, which those who tend to bemoan lamping may possess.

Lamping hares with dogs does lend itself to larger numbers being able to be accounted for. On a dayight mooch we may only see and chase one or two hares, on the lamping stage a greater number will always be witnessed and possibly ran. Hare when being chased by dogs, especially on the lamp, are a mixture of stupidity and intelligence, even during daytime racing of hares this is evident. How many people have seen their dogs chasing a fleeing hare and looking like getting nowhere near, then for some unexplained reason the hare stops, as if letting the dog catch up. I know I have.

Two lamping hunters maneuvering hares between them should ultimately secure decent bags of brown hares, and for the aspiring profit hunter this is what it is all about, catching not just exercising the creature. Some folk say that they like to see the hare get away after a good, long exciting course. For me this is "rubbish". After a long tiring course the last thing I want to witness is the hare getting away. My duty of care is to my dogs, not the hare, the All Mother looks after hers and I look after mine, and I much prefer witnessing my dogs succeed, rather than fail.

Blue hares

It was in the mid-seventies when I first heard of lurcherlads from my area travelling over the borders and racing blue hares. Some of

Brown hares.

these guys, now highly respected in hare coursing circles, told stories of these "formiddable creatures" that were fleet of foot, and more difficult to catch with lurchers than their brown counterparts. At this time we believed these tales until we had the opportunity to test them with our own dogs.

Petrol was cheap at this time, in fact pre-decimalisation I remember a time when eight gallons could be bought for a pound. One weekend a few of us decided to fill the tank of our Triumph 2000 TC and head off over the border in search of some sport. On the day we shot over 80 rabbits from the car window with air rifles, mostly on grass verges at the side of the roads we travelled on, including the A1. We went through areas and villages possessing such interesting names as Reston, Quixwood, Abbey St Bathams, Cockburnspath, Spott and Longframacus. We travelled slowly up on to the Lammermuir Hills and this is where we had the first opportunity to race these blue hares.

The first hare we laid eyes upon was just off the roadside of the single road that snakes through the Lammermiurs. This creature was mostly white in colour, but with patches of grey and fawn, making it almost harlaquin like. The brakes of the car where slammed on, the three dogs on the back seat not wearing seat belts almost came over into the front of the car. The passenger side door was opened and the first dog out was Bes.

Now, Bes was what I have always considered to be the best all round lurcher I have ever owned, or indeed witnessed. Doubting her ability on rabbit, brown hare, fox and deer had never been part of any Barbour jacket I had worn. But these were blue hares, "formiddable" creatures whose ability and agility abounds, prey that were so difficult to be taken by previous hunting teams from Ashington.

Bes wasn't a big dog, standing 23.5 inches at the shoulder, and weighing 45lb when fit. She sailed across this ocean of heather akin to a stately Spanish galleon dipping through the tropics by palm green shores, a situate where I have since witnessed many smaller dogs getting a bit bogged down. Her nose was almost touching the tail of the fleeing creature within seconds. A couple of jinks and the creatures death screams rang out above the haunting cries of curlews across this tranquil moorland setting. Bes was a natural retriever, and after killing her hare she was working her way back towards us, her neck pushing towards the indigo skies so the hanging hare didn't get hampered in the heather. Suddenly another hare lifted from it's seat and Bes dropped her hare and set off after the second. Again

The author with brown and, below, blue hares.

similar to the first run, the hare was taken after a short run.

"What the hell had these other guys been talking about," I thought to myself. Maybe we had just bumped into the worst two blue hares residing on the Lammermuirs, aged or infirmed individuals that couldn't physically exhibit what a fit, healthy hare is supposed to show. No we hadn't, and on the first excursion we took over 30 blue hares with three dogs.

Over many decades I've travelled over the Anglo Scottish border to take blue hares, and I've never had a dog that could do the business on them. Even the deerhounds my father and I possessed in the 90s caught these creatures that boasted the proud name of hare, but at times in running abilities acted like rabbits. Some of our hounds taking double figures in a day's sport.

Shooting hares

Hares for me are animals that just shouldn't be shot, but, yes I have taken a few over the years with air rifles from the window of a car. I was also invited by a gamekeeper friend to a hare shoot, two days of hare slaughter, where 300 hares were shot on the first day, and 301 on the second day. Numbers you might think that would excite the profit hunter, but for the first time in my life I felt glum after being out in the fields.

Even the times when I participated in shooting hares from the car window with my air rifle, yes it secured numbers, but for me it was never my favoured past-time, and this was an era I quickly grew out of.

Snaring hares

For me, snaring is the worst of all hunting methods, and snaring hares is unforgiveable. There will be others who differ with my opinion, and that's fine, however only a few lines will be devoted in this book as I possess little experience in this field and could never profit from being involved in any form or guise with the practice of snaring.

Gate netting hares

It was my father who first educated me to the fact that hares could be taken in the daylight and during the hours of darkness with the aid of the gate net. It was also my mentor who taught me how to knit these devices, nets that were made in square mesh, not the diamond mesh that I had earlier been taught to manufacture.

When I first began to practice using gate nets, this took place mainly during the day. Many of the gates to farmers' fields in those

Deerhounds coursing hares on the fens.

days were made of wood, so too were the posts on which they hung. Our nets were hung in such a way, drapped from post to post so that they would come away with the force of the hare hitting the net. The creature would then be ensnared in the hemp net's grip. Using a gate net was extremely useful when coursing a hare next to a road, as nine times out of ten the fleeing hare will always work the dog back towards the gate. Without the opening being netted, both dog and hare could end up running on the road's hard surface, and this would ultimately end up with the dog's pads of its feet being burst, and the dog rendered useless in some case for a number of weeks. I have witnessed dogs working with various cuts and knocks, but even the hardest of lurchers will not perform with cuts or Chinees type burns to their pads.

On one occasion while coursing a hare near St Mary's Hospital near Stannington beside Morpeth, it was fairly latish to be still illegally coursing hares, but we just couldn't resist a course on the way home from one of Lord Ridley's estate invitations. Low and behold the hare broke onto the main road with two dogs close behind. Billy Wright (Spike) saw what was going to happen, and he also spotted the old Bedford school bus chugging along on its way to pick the local farmers' kids up. Spike ran out the gate and onto the road, putting his hand up like a traffic warden, stopping the bus. The bewildered driver sat in amazement as a hare and dogs shot out of the gate, crossed the road and entered the field on the other side of the road. Spike waved the bus to pass, and we watched the ensuing course and subsequent kill.

During the 90s a friend of mine had some very good ground that housed a lot of hares, and with the farmer's permission we regularly coursed our lurchers there. This area too was close to main roads, and we often gate netted hares to stop our dogs getting injured or even hit by oncoming traffic.

Later I did try nocturnal excursions gate netting hares with dogs, however I am no dog trainer and the number of times attempting this pastime was limited.

Longnetting hares

It was on hilly ground north of the border where we first tried this activity out, an area we knicknamed the "Plato" because at the top of rolling hills the fields actually leveled off, and this long-grassed short-heathered area housed hundreds of rabbits, and we had many record breaking nights' sport there. After securing big bags of rabbits we would head back to the hidden vehicle, cutting across large short cropped fields on bank sides absolutely heaving with hares. We often raced these beasts, but due to the fact that we had just caught over 100 rabbits, the fields being on banks and possessing short cropped grass akin to a golf course didn't stack the odds in the profit hunters' favour for securing large numbers of the co habitors of these fields.

We came up with the idea of using a longnet to obtain the numbers that would excite us. But not using these devices in the traditional way.

Our idea was to set the net in the form of an arc, from the dry stone wall, semi-circled out into the field and back towards the wall, with a gateway in the middle. We then walked along a track which took us to the bottom edge of this very large field. We then worked the field with lamps and dogs back up towards the top corner of the field, where the gate, and beyond the longnet was waiting in ambush. Profit hunting outings at times can be likened to military maneuvers.

On the way we sometimes accounted for kills by expertly working the hares towards each other. Closer and closer we walked towards the top gate. Getting there we went into the next field to check our net. That first evening there was nine hares caught up in the net, quite a decent haul. We used this ploy many times over the years, with our biggest haul being a dozen hares.

I always think that the worst thing when catching a large number of hares is the actual carrying of them. They are bigger than rabbits, and in some cases can weigh three times as much, and the way I hang them on myself to carry ensures that their heads continually back against my knee when walking, and if they have been taken with dogs, they bleed profusely, leaving jeans or trousers soaked in blood. But hey ho, I would rather have blood stained clothes and sore knees than not.

Hare in our locality were always more difficult to sell than rabbits, but at some times of the year we secured £3 a hare from old Hursty, as well as the profit hunter obtaining vast enjoyment and sport, different forms of sport at times I must admit when longnetting the beast, but sport never the less.

CHAPTER 14

"I Am a Game Dealer, My Father Was a Game Dealer"

T HE BEST game-dealers that shall we say, I have worked with, were individuals who never mixed the vocations of game dealing with game keeping, and who were, for want of a healthier term, "bent".

In over 30 years I must have flogged a large percentage of my spoils to around 12 different game dealers, from Duns to Durham, and of these "dirty dozen" only two could be classed as being experts in their fields. In all this time only one individual gained my total trust and more importantly, respect, and that was "Old Hursty" who operated in Newcastle's Green Market.

The Green Market began as an informal open-air market outside St Andrew's church on Newgate Street in the heart of the city. Towards the end of the 19th century it moved to buildings at Green Court, and it was here where the game dealing company of Warner and Hurst bought and sold game.

As a child I can vividly remember my father taking me to such places, and how we stood on a carpet of sawdust staring in thrilling wonderment at rows of hanging rabbits, game birds of every description and full roe deer carcasses. The smell that excited my young olfactory senses was not that of death, but of sheer unadulterated excitement. Little did I realise at this time that one day it would be some of my hunting proceeds that would be on full display for the next generation of Northumberland hunters to gaze upon.

For many years the main quarry we hunted was rabbits, and this poor man's meat was relatively easy to sell in the local pubs and clubs. Our ploy on selling days was to order our drinks then one of us would approach a table of men sitting in conversation or playing games of cards or dominos.

"Anyone want any rabbits?"

There was always at least one taker. This was just the first phase, can you see where its leading?

"How much?"

"A pound a couple."

The rabbits were brought into the building in full view, not in bags or wrapped in newspaper. Inquisitive eyes stared intensely at the delivery men ferrying coney, payments were passed over and the deal was done, then it began.

A constant supply of men asking, "Got any rabbits left youngin?" until our haul was completely exhausted.

Rabbits remained my main quarry for the rest of my life, but opportunities for the taking of almost every other prey species came knocking, and when they did, not only did the doors open for these to excite my hunting nature, but they temporarily altered my whole ethos around poaching.

Lurchers with deer.

With bigger volumes of rabbits, and good numbers of the likes of hare, roe deer, salmon and game birds the buzz sought from my clandestine endeavours increased. But now there was the added opportunity of financial gain to a degree never experienced before, to supplement the poor wages as a motor mechanic, and to pay for the likes of my young family's Christmas presents. Had it not been for the extra money coming in from poaching at times we would have gone without things that most families now take for granted, and this includes food. To put this modern day hardship into perspective, during one particular hard time in the late 1970s the only thing in our house to consume was tea bags. My wife and I searched down the backs of the chairs and sofa and found enough money to purchase a couple of Kit Kats from the corner shop, to us at that time this was a godsend and that afternoon we ate like kings and queens.

With numbers of rabbits per night consistently passing the 100 mark, hares taken with dogs or nets regularly reaching double figures in one outing, deer being taken like never before and not to mention at certain times of the year pheasant and partridges being accounted for up to 100 plus per night, a new problem had arose, where to get rid of the plunder. This was also a time before most people relied on freezers, tools of the rich folk to bulk buy and stock up on luxury food items.

So this is where my associations with game dealers partly began, a safe outlet to take all, or even part of our spoils, and what better game dealer to highlight than Newcastle's Warner and Hurst, and the old grey haired man, wearing glasses and always donning a tweed suit, collar and tie.

Illicit proceeds of poaching trips were always delivered to Hursty at an old brick built processing plant, veiled by a natural cloaking device of broad leaved bushes on the rural outskirts of Gosforth near Newcastle, where only a tall, rickety chimney gave away this most unlikely hiding place. On every visit the old man's proud voice would proclaim, "I am a game dealer, my father was a game dealer and his father before him was a game dealer".

Never have I met a man so proud of his working heritage, a gentleman who rose early, worked late and in the hours between never let up. A most knowledgeable man indeed in the realms of game.

Yes, Hursty was a workaholic, but his working ethos ensured he knew everything there was to know about the birds and beasts that he worked so closely and intimately with, an enthusiasm that demonstrated respect, a reverence that ensured that carcases were treated appropriately at all times and that nothing was ever wasted. My life has many similarities with the philosophies of this man, I possess a natural abhorrence of waste and would never kill anything just for the sake of it, a culture lacking in many so-called hunters.

Hursty talked to me like a man, and treated me like a grandson. The highest accolade this man bestowed upon me was on a day when he put his arm around me and said in a voice of measured grandiloquence, "You are the most respectful person that brings game to me, I admire the way you treat the creatures you bring, it's always a pleasure to do business with you young man."

Hursty was as fair a man as he was a gentleman. His fairness was shown to me many times, and one occasion in particular. I had taken a roe deer buck with one of my dogs, Kit. Now Kit was only 24 inches at the shoulder but she was a demon lurcher on the back of a deer, where she showed the creature no mercy when her bite sank into bulging haunches. She possessed so much ability on this prey that when she was slipped on a roe, you just expected her to get it, and I was totally flabbergasted if she failed. This deer had been mauled, and at one point I was contemplating feeding it to the dogs. I phoned Hursty, and he gave me a remarkable choice.

"Bring it over and leave it, I will strip it and see what I can salvage and will give you a price, if you're not happy with the price, you can take all the clean, jointed meat for yourself."

Well, how could anyone refuse such an offer? On phoning him up from work the next morning the offer was £27, which I accepted and picked the money up three weeks later when I had 140 partridges to weigh in.

Another time the old fellow warned us that the police were getting fairly hot on people bringing in illegally taken game, especially venison. He had to take the names and addresses of anyone bringing deer to the factory. We took three roe deer to him shortly after this apologetic warning, Hursty weighed the deer, and worked out the price. From a drawer he took a brown official looking book that he had been instructed to use, licked the tip of his pencil before writing, looked me in the eye and said with an air of sarcasm in his voice.

"The name is Smith isn't it, and is it Blyth where you live?"

This was Hursty, always a business man as well as a game dealer.

Pre-Hursty era I always skinned and jointed any deer that my dogs caught, and did this similarly to jointing a rabbit, ending up with the two back legs, the saddle, and two front legs. One day I boyishly asked Hursty if he would demonstrate how to joint a deer properly. The old man promptly rolled up his sleeves placed the deer I had just taken in on his butchering slab, skinned it and showed me every joint, every cut possible to make full use of this most wonderful tasting meat.

Many game dealers I've been involved with always seemed to dwell over how to sex partridges, more in their favour I would hasten to add, as there has always been a large difference between the prices of young birds to the price of old birds. Hursty would simply go along the lines of laid out birds, move them about a bit, and then give you his accurate number, "60 young and 40 old birds my friend".

Many of his contemporaries I have witnessed spreading the wing feathers, blowing the breast feathers, examining the bird's legs, beaks, head shape, tail flights and probably every other part of the bird's anatomy. Amateurs!

An Ashington game dealer did his gender decision making totally by the shape of the bird's main flights, a pointed flight meant a young bird, and well-rounded flights indicated old birds. To trick this man who regularly cheated us, we made a solution of water and sugar, then dipped all the ends of the bird wing feathers in this, and pulled and shaped the tips to form points. This did the trick for a time, until he got wary and started weighing the birds, each bird having to meet a desired weight, and any birds that didn't were priced down. How many bolts and screws were pushed into the partridges through their back passage to bump up their weight is nobody's business. At times one has to fight fire with fire.

A future profit hunter, possibly!

Hares too were also subject to the Ashington game fiddler's scrutiny of how heavy they were, and even more nuts and bolts were obtained from the stores at work, it's a good job he didn't put the game we delivered to him under an electro magnet.

As I have mentioned earlier, waste and I just don't squander anything when it comes to the creatures I have hunted, and following this ethos apart from the meat to be consumed by either humans or the dogs, many of the otherwise discarded items such as skins, feathers and other body parts were used, again mimicking what I had witnessed at Hursty's.

The old man had tea chests where the down stripped from ducks was collected and stored. There where containers full of bundled up pheasants' tail feathers, hare masks, partridge wings and cut up squares of roe deer skin all treated with borax to be later sold for anglers' fly tying purposes. Skins from rabbits were sent to West Highland Furs, nothing whatsoever was wasted.

I practiced taxidermy for many years and some of the items that did well for me Hursty took on board, he would sell some of these items, and of course, like his father before him made a profit in the process. Walking sticks with roe deer's feet for the handle, mounted hares' heads and a mount where a pheasant's back area with tail was cured then fixed to a wooden base and the neck and head also cured and mounted on top of the tail section. Hursty loved these and had them hanging up all over his factory unit for decoration and of course, for sale.

As with the Albino gypsy, my life wouldn't have been complete without the input from my associations with old Hursty.

The factory unit has been long gone, and the elderberry bushes which circumnavigated the building and provided goldfinches with five star accommodation have been pulled up making way for roads and houses, but to those of us who had dealings with this old man the memory of time spent delivering game, chatting and listening to his offerings will last forever. Whenever I think of old Hursty his catch phrase immediately enters my mind through the mists of the past, "I am a game dealer, my father was a game dealer and his father before him was a game dealer."

RIP old friend.

CHAPTER 15

Bes

THE UNMISTAKEABLE stale smell of afterbirth filled the kennel and the remains of amniotic sacs lay tangled amid the barley straw bed where a lurcher bitch still with puppies to come took a short rest from pushing and panting. She was now weak with her labours, and even raising her head required a strength that her tired body could barely provide. Shortly another whelp entered this world, helped by the strong but careful hands of the bitches' owner.

"There's one for the sweep," he said uninterestingly, at the same time almost throwing the pup into the awaiting loins of the exhausted bitch. Yes, the pup was small, but in no way was this diminutive lurcher a runt or a crit. From day one she fought with all her bigger siblings; she pushed her way to the front against dogs much stronger than herself. Unwanted for the first 12 weeks of her life, she eventually ended up with me, and she became the best all-round lurcher I have ever possessed or witnessed. This was Bes.

Fifteen pounds was the asking price for the pup, quite a pricey sum in those days for a lurcher pup. The vendor and I visited my dad to get him to cast his critical eye over the dog, to see what he thought before I parted with any hard earned cash. In the confines of the living room the pup ran around the settee like a greyhound on a flapping track, with the occasional leap on to the soft cushions, and the odd role over on her back peeing over my mother's carpet through sheer excitement.

Bes with a hare.

My dad sat watching the pup, observing her every move eventually lifting his jumper and the pup, as if commanded, dived onto my dad's chest. Dad covered her up with his jumper, the bitch pushed her head through the collar and pushed her long black muzzle up against my dad's face and lay there tired, but completely settled.

"I think she is a lovely animal," said dad. "If you don't take her, I will."

I paid the boy, dropped him off on the way home and thus began a friendship between dog and man that lasted over 13 years. As with all love affairs however, our bond was not without its ups and downs, and here dear reader is a brief synopsis of our magical time together.

Although I had hunted with many dogs in the past, this was the first lurcher that I had ever actually owned, the first lurcher that was mine. Not that I didn't want a lurcher during my hunting apprenticeship, the time just couldn't have been right. I am a great believer of fate, that all things happen for a reason. It was now time for me to have my dog.

My dad was a great dog man, whippets were primarily his favourite dog, and he raced them at the many local sweeps at that time, but he also hunted with these wee dogs, on rabbits and the occasional strong Northumberland hare. Dad helped me rear Bes from this point, ordering me to give her things to eat to assist her development, items that I had never even heard of before.

For my part, I could have easily undone all the hard work, as I was anxious to get her out, to kill rabbits and hares akin to the dogs belonging to the boys I was travelled with. This was a time before lamping, so it was ferreting and mooching for rabbits and going out in the early mornings for hares, traveling along roads through the game abundant countryside of mid to north Northumberland that were the main hunting activities.

Bes was immediately taken out on early morning hare coursing jaunts. Experienced dogs were slipped from the car on strong hares. I grabbed Bes on each occasion, holding her in my arms allowing her to observe the spectacle, her strong heart pounding like a drum in the palm of my hand. Bes relished this, even though she was a bad traveller, and was sick almost every time I took her in the car. Bes learnt some of her trade watching an excellent hare coursing machine of a dog, Drum, owned by my good friend Davey Gibson, both who unfortunately are no longer with us.

Bes was just over four months when impatience got the better of me and I slipped her on a squatting hare. Now before the oohs and arrhs of shock horror, I know, I've scolded myself and countless others for this or similar stupidity over the years many times.

On the morning Drum was already coursing another hare in the same field, but my eyes where focused on Bes, and I was amazed how well my little bitch did on the back of this formidable creature she pursued. Bes didn't bark nor give in and eventually lost the hare when it got through a fence and into some long corn. This was to be one of the positive traits of this bitch's running style, she would never gave in. Drum got his hare and even Davey's tunnel vision of his own dog's prowess was directed at how well Bes had performed.

Although Davey was my mate, later in my bitch's coursing career he did spoil the opportunity of Bes getting her first hare at the ripe old age of six months ... I know! I will tire of apologizing for the mistakes I will document while bringing up this lurcher.

I spotted a hare squatting amid some longish grass in fields at Prewick Carrs near Newcastle airport, an ideal opportunity for my young bitch. I walked Bes on a slip leader towards the crouching animal which was getting smaller the closer I got to it, almost digging

Old Bes.

itself into its warm form. The hare was now nervous at our approach and was twitching and ready to burst from her resting place. Closer and closer we got, Gibson was a fair way behind me with Drum, also on his slip. The hare lifted and Bes was released. Before the hare could get into top gear Bes tumbled the hare. Get in, her first hare, I thought. Gibson in his infinite wisdom slipped Drum, and he charged in like a rhino to take the hare from the grasp of my bitch's mouth. Bes was startled and the hare was released and the course was on, and what a course it was, probably more deserving than the almost "kick up" earlier, the hare showing why we call these creatures the ultimate quarry at times, jinking and turning between the two dogs. What a show young Bes put up against the animal that didn't want to have dog's teeth in its flesh again. Bes also showed an excellent performance against an experienced dog that until then I believed to be one of the best hare dogs I had seen. The hare escaped, and I threw every epithet of damnation at Gibson in that field and I didn't speak to him all the way home.

Bes caught her first hare proper when she was 10 months, and until that age she had less than 20 rabbits under her belt. Then lamping arrived, lighting the blue touch paper to a poaching firework that exploded on to the Northumberland hunting scene like a Roman candle, and for me a past-time that was to almost take over my life.

Before her initiation into the nocturnal world of lamping, Bes led me and my family a merry dance. Until now she had been a house dog, and with that all the trials and tribulations associated with keeping a dog in your home: messing in the house, chewing the furniture, howling the place down when I was at work and killing my wife's budgie. Who would think a dog would put such a strain on a marriage, and it did, and looking back expecting my wife to accept what was happening was totally selfish. Then during a heated argument over a pine table totally destroyed, I did the unthinkable. Bes was thrown into my black Hillman Avenger taken to the neighboring township of Morpeth and dropped off in the middle of a housing estate. The thought of that little dog running after a car that wasn't going to slow down still haunts me to this day, and a deed that brings tears to my eyes as I write.

That morning I went straight to work from Morpeth, unable to think straight, or to focus on the tasks of my employment. The eight hour shift seemed like a life sentence.

On getting home I broke down and cried like a baby as I explained to my wife what I had done. My wife although angry at what the dog had done, consoled me during the despair that drove me to tears.

"Go and get her, see if she's still there," she said tearfully.

Like a La Mans racing driver I leapt into the car and sped away to find my dog. Frantically I searched the streets, slowing down at every yard between every house. Some kids were playing on a small piece of grass at the end of one of the lanes, and I stopped the car and beckoned one of them over.

"Hey youngin, have you seen a little black dog knocking about?" The lad stood there with his size five caser under his arm and a snot as long as my little finger hanging from his nose.

"There was one around there before," and he pointed in the direction of where he had seen her.

Around a couple of corners and into a cul de sac, and there, following some other children was Bes, her tail wagging as if she was enjoying herself, greeding sweets from kids with more heart than I showed earlier in the day. Instantly I was overwhelmed with joy, excitement rushed through my body as I drove towards her.

"Bes, Bes," I yelled getting out the car. The dog turned, I would have forgiven her if she had just kept on walking with her new chums,

Bes and pups.

but she didn't. She ran to me and almost knocked me off my feet. I had my dog back, and I never let this faithful companion down again. A new shed was bought and erected in my garden, and as if Bes knew what had caused the trouble in the first place never put a foot wrong ever again.

Bes as a hunter adjusted instantly to the rigors of lamping. The first time I took her out I borrowed a lamp and battery, and my evening consisted of driving country lanes at around eight at night, stopping and shining into fields at every gateway. Hares were taken frequently using this method, and I went out almost every night of the week, back in the house by midnight with my spoils, I just couldn't get enough of seeing my dog hunting.

Gibson and I bought motorbike batteries and made lamps, using Lucas square eights robbed off buses that we worked on. We began to travel further afield, to areas where we previously hunted with longnets. These were rabbit-infested areas, and we enjoyed some exciting times lamping there, and Bes blossomed and flourished with the extra demand bestowed upon her, raising her to a level unmatched by any of the dogs travelling with us at this time.

Rabbits were taken in quanities unheard of before with dogs. Where once we were getting twos and threes per week with our dogs, lamping was allowing us to take 10s, 20s and in Bes's case 30s in a single night's graft. This was stuff dreams are made of.

Bes was 23.5 inches at the shoulder, she weighed around 45lb when fit, so first impressions would suggest she was a rabbit dog, but first impressions were only partly correct. Yes, she was a demon rabbiter, and not only during the daylight hours where she was one of the few dogs locally during that era that authentically took over a thousand rabbits. Hares also remained a creature that Bes excelled on, and not restricted to the lamp, Bes took over 100 hares in her time, this not including the blues hares that she killed. As a hare killer I can categorically say that in all the times she coursed, day or night, I never witnessed a dog better her in the field behind a hare.

Did her diminutive size stop her from taking bigger game? Did it hell as like. Bes was a slow starter on roe deer, more due to my thinking she wouldn't be able to manage these beasts than to her ability. Once she got a taste of chasing and catching these creatures, she became quite an expert at it. On stuff that bites back, well I've never been a person for these, but every dog I've owned, including Bes took these, and the biggest fox I ever caught with a dog was killed at fields next to Tranwell Wood singularly handled by Bes.

Bes as a producer passed on many of her most useful traits to her offspring, and she was the foundation bitch that begat the line that I had in the future for many decades, all grafters, every one a 110% all-round worker.

Bes ran till she was over 13 years old, from the age of 12 I gave her the odd half a dozen rabbits every now and then, just to keep her fit, and quiet. Taking her daughters or her granddaughters out and leaving Bes at home in the kennel was a recipe for a noisy evening for my wife and neighbours.

I have attempted to condense 13 years of this dog's life into one chapter, an impossible literary feat to achieve, what do I put in, what do I leave out? I have however, managed to give a brief insight into the history of this animal, a canine autobiography that could fill every page of a book totally devoted to a little dog with a heart like a lion that I loved so much. Bes, a lurcher that never knew what it was like to give in.

CHAPTER 16

Kit

MY NAME is Kit. I'm a lurcher, a hunting dog, and I cannot think of any other breed of dog I would rather be. My entire life was a wonderful time with my master, a time of continual hunting, at times with my parents, Bes and Paddy, who both taught me a great deal, watching them chasing hares, rabbits, deer and fox in the dark and also running in the daytime. Sometimes I also hunted with some of my brothers, sisters, kennel friends and my uncle Blue.

My master expertly guided me from when I was a pup to full grown, and I remember him telling me how to do things, stuff that my mother advised me that the "master knows best", and that we should always do what he wanted us to do. Once my master told his friend I was the best deer dog he had ever seen, and I was so proud of what he said, but remember my dad Paddy taking a bit of a huff over it. My mother Bes took a lot of pride over what our master said, and I could feel this pleasure oozing from her as we lay snugly together on a warm bed of straw. Yes I'm just a dog, but I also have many tales to tell, and I would love you to read at least some of my story.

Firstly, my birth place was a wooden shed at the bottom of my master's garden. It may sound silly but I can vividly remember entering this world; even though I couldn't hear or see what was going on around me at that time. I did feel things wriggling beside me, these felt nice and I relished being next to them. They felt so warm and my senses told me that no harm would come to me with these other things sharing the shed, and something told me not to leave these, and to

Me and my mam.

remain as close as possible to them, and my little strong legs pushed continuously so our bodies were almost as one.

Apart from these warm wrigglers, I sensed a most wondrous presence very close by, much bigger than those who continually squashed against me. A presence that left me feeling so safe, a maternal magnet that drew me to it no matter if I was sleeping or if awake, it was my lovely mother, Bes. With all these things beside me I felt so much contentment and joy, and also so safe there in their presence.

At regular intervals there was also a most horrible feeling, a sickly sensation that made me suffer, a feeling that awoke me from my slumber and caused panic to run riot through every part of my young body. At these times my mother sensing my ailing would gently nuzzle me towards her. I moved guided at times only by a strange sense giving me direction, and once there she offered me sustenance in the form of the milk she kept just for us. Oh how wonderful this milk tasted, a beautiful flavour for which superlatives will never truly be able to describe. We drank like miners at a broth day, till eventually the horrible feeling left, and sleep led me to a wondrous seductive dreamland.

At about four days old I felt being picked up as I had been a number of times, even at this age my nose could detect different smells, and this allowed me to detect a most unusual odour, "human breath" we dogs call it. My master tends to remember things by giving them names, or by using numbers, how weird is that, us dogs remember all the important things by their different smells, a much easier way.

This time being picked up, however, the odour was followed by pain, a hurt never felt before. An unbearable, excruciating hurt that made me cry out and feel so scared, I called out loudly for my mother. Seconds later, and again the same pain. I struggled and fought but felt clamped and helpless, then suddenly I was next to my mother again who sniffed and licked me continuously, a soothing nurturing that helped me endure the frightening experience. Into sleep I fell, whimpering and crying.

A week or so had passed since the pain, but what a red letter day this was to be. My eyes were now open and I could see, I could also hear, what a magical day indeed. For the first time I was able to see my lovely mother, the most beautiful face in the entire world staring

My brothers and sisters.

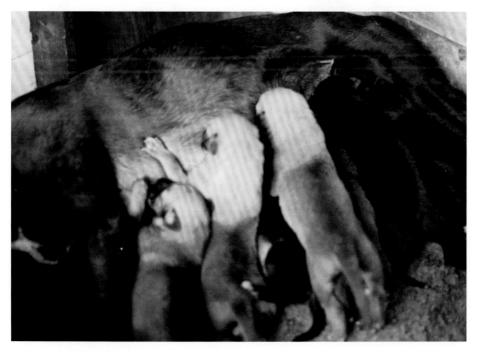

down at me proudly. Her short hair was so black it was almost silver as shafts of daylight through the window of the shed played upon her. Her kind eyes were big, wide and lustrous and her ears were pricked and alert looking, listening intensely to every squeak her children made. My mother's ears then pinned back to her head, she pushed me over on to my back and licked and licked at my belly, so tickly this felt that I actually peed myself.

Suddenly there was another sight bestowed upon me, no time to dawdle it was a time of exploration. The wrigglers next to me also had faces, some were black like my mother's, not as shiny, more of a grey cast to it, others were a sort of brown colour, they too could now see and we formally introduced one another. My siblings consisted of five brothers and two sisters, and over the weeks we chased each other with our mum watching. We played and tumbled till we could chase no more. So tired, but so content we made our way back to the shed where we flopped into the sanctuary of our mother's inviting loins.

Day by day my strength grew, stronger and stronger. More and more with my brothers and sisters we fought and tumbled, chased

Me.

148

and battled. We were all still drinking my mother's milk, but I noticed that she was eating things given to her by my master. One day, when no one was looking I tried to eat this too, a small amount that had been dropped, and my mother got very angry. Later however, my master gave me something to eat, it was quite difficult to swallow, and afterwards my stomach ached and rumbled and I farted all through the night, but the food was nice to taste, my master said it was "rabbit's kidneys". Every so often my master gave me lots of new things to taste, until one day when calling in for a drink from my mother there was nothing there, harder and harder my lips sucked, my tongue curled around the feeder but still nothing was forthcoming. I sucked till my mother got very angry, growling at me to show her displeasure, and never again did my lips engulf what was once my life line, the soft pink nipple that ensured the commencement of my life was the best possible start.

One day my master visited us with another human. This person picked me up, but not in the same way as my master did. Those hand things were very rough, they smelt like they had been on fire, and they threw me about, and those long finger things probed and prodded me, even opening my mouth, it was like having a giant cigar in my mouth. This person said, "Al tek this un". I wasn't sure what these words meant, but they didn't sound very nice, and the tone they were said in was cold and demanding. Then I felt the warm gentle grip of my master holding me, and him saying, "Sorry matie, this one is not for sale". These words sounded much nicer, but firm.

Sadly one of my sisters left us, and I never saw her again. This happened more times over the next few weeks until it was just me and my mother left in our draft free home, it did give us more space to stretch out and sleep comfortably, but for a short time sadness reigned in our once happy shed, my mind constantly wondering whatever happened to the siblings that had come into the world with me. The comfort knowing that my master would not have let my brothers and sisters go to a place where they would be harmed reassured us and rocked us back to cheerfulness.

This was a time of change, when my master would bring presents to me, only for him then to throw them away. My mother must have thought these were nice and she ran after them and brought them back. My master mustn't have really wanted to loose them, as he praised my mam and cuddled her for returning them. But then he threw them away again. Strange guy my master.

My mother then got her "neck squeezer" put on her, and my master again threw the round thing he had brought. I remember how she pulled wanting to get it back for him, but she couldn't. So my mam wouldn't be upset, I ran after it and brought it back. My master was very, very pleased, he patted me, cuddled me and even gave me something to eat, something very nice I remember, something called "a piece of cheese".

My master, mother and me did this lots and lots of times, until he only did it with me, I think he realised mother was getting on a bit and she might need a rest, I can live with that. He didn't just throw these round things. One day he threw a strange hairy thing called a rabbit.

This thing didn't bounce or roll akin to my usual toys; it just landed limply with a dull thud. As usual I ran after it, but when sniffing this thing apprehension flooded through the whole of my body. What was it? It didn't just look different, it smelt different, and when gripped in my mouth it felt different, something inside me was telling me to bite it as hard as I could. My teeth sank into this rabbit in a pleasant way; this was a nice feeling, its soft fur felt nice on the ribbed roof of my mouth. Suddenly my master's voice was shouting my name, and also the word he always shouted when he thought he had lost what he had thrown.

"Kit, fetch, Kit, fetch." I picked up this rabbit thing and took it back to my master. He was very pleased. Looking over towards my mam, her eyes were smiling so endearingly towards me, her head cocked slightly to one side so proud she looked, I ran towards her and our cold noses touched, and we played all the way home, oh how happy we were in those halcyon days.

My master is such a funny person, but I love him so much. It's not only the things he does, like making out he is a dog by him and my mistress putting their lips together, touching noses, I'm sure they are just copying me and my mam. He also says such funny things. Often I have heard him saying that he is so tired when he comes in from the place he calls "work". Then when he should be asleep in bed he knocks me and my mother up and we go out in the dark till its nearly light again, then he goes back to that work place. Us dogs would never say or do that, if we are tired we sleep, if we are hungry we clear our food bowls, I remember my master saying he was starving, and he didn't eat all his food, leaving loads that he gave to me and my mam. Curious animals these humans!

Over the months we did many new activities together, until one night when we should have been in bed, my master knocked us up and we went out for a long journey in the back of his car. It was late, and we travelled a long way, at first I stood up and watched lots of bright lights coming towards us in the darkness, until my legs got tired and I lay next to my mother who was curled up fast asleep.

Then we stopped, it was dark when we all go out of the car, I was bursting for the toilet and had to have a pee. Our master took us into this new place through a wooden gate. A bright light was put on and there were lots of those rabbit things, but, my master didn't throw them, they were actually running themselves, how the hell do they do that?

I pulled excitedly to run after them to play and bite them, but I couldn't escape the grip of the neck squeezer, my mother mustn't have had hers on, as she ran after the rabbit. Never had I seen my mother run as fast, even at times when we played in the fields next to our home. Quickly she caught the rabbit up and picked it up in her mouth. The rabbit squealed, my mother must have been a little too rough with this toy, then suddenly silence reigned; my mother brought the rabbit back and gave it to my master. He was very pleased with her, and speaking in a voice of grandiloquence said, "Well done old girl."

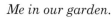

Me in our garden.

Over a dozen times my mother chased the rabbits, every time I wished and preyed that it was my turn next, it looked so much fun. The light went on again, a rabbit was running, but this time there was no holding me back by my neck squeezer. My master called out, "Go on Kit."

With this new found freedom I ran as fast as my legs could carry me, but these rabbits were fast, not as easy as my mother had made them look, and at that point I didn't think I could catch up. I tried even harder and this time found myself getting up to it so much easier. I was just going to grab it, but the little beggar turned and went the other way, I had to stop as quickly as possible and started chasing it again. This rabbit mustn't have wanted to be caught like the ones that my mother had taken earlier. Time and time it jinked and turned, this was a great game, "wheeeee". Then as I got to it this time it didn't turn, and it was in my mouth. The pleasurable feeling of my teeth sinking into rabbit flesh came flooding back and my teeth bit hard. The rabbit cried out, and I nearly dropped it in fright. The rabbit struggled and my teeth sank in again, then, silence, the creature went limp in my mouth, and nice tasting rabbit juice ran over my bottom jaw.

Over the top of the angry song that the wind was singing, my master's voice called my name, "Kit, Kit, fetch it."

Quickly I took it back for my master, never had I seen him as happy, he cuddled me, and even kissed me on the side of the face, I licked his face, how I love my master. My master let me chase and catch rabbits a few more times that evening, and in the proceeding years many more rabbits were chased, and the more I caught, the easier they seemed to get.

My master also took me and my mother out in the daytime chasing these rabbits. This wasn't as exciting as it was at night, and we never chased as many, and at night there were always more natural sounds to listen to, rather than those noisy car things echoing in the distance. In the day time however, we did meet some nice friendly guys, hunting chums called ferrets by my master. These were always good to be out with, and their crack was good, but by god did they stink.

Also during the day my master took me to chase something else, hares he called them. Apart from having better smell, hearing and sight than my master, I also have better senses that can detect when things are not quite right. On the morning of my first run on a hare, my finely honed senses were telling me that things were not quite right with my master, the confidence I detected from him every time I ran was not there, he was quieter, there was doubt in his words, I was worried about how this would effect his performance on the morning.

In the field he let me off the leader, and my mother and I ran about excitedly exploring all the thrilling smells our noses detected. My nose was close to the ground, and out of the corner of my eyes I could see my mother was working hard. Suddenly mam's tail pointed stiffly towards the steel grey sky, side to side it stiffly waved. Mam called to me in the way only us dogs can between each other. My master's voiced blasted out, "Bes Kit."

I turned and my mother was already running, but this was no rabbit, it looked like a rabbit, but it was much bigger, much stronger and certainly faster. The smell from it was also sweeter than that of the smaller rabbits, an odour that overwhelmed me, pressing every button of excitement that my body and mind possessed, turning on every switch of stimulation.

Never had I witnessed a creature run as fast as this, my young mind could never conjure up a pen profile to match what my eyes were so lucky to be spectator to.

Mam ran this animal across the grassy running stage, but every time she was going to catch it, the bloody thing jinked or turned in attempts to shake my mam off. I ran behind, trying to catch up. A sharp turn and my mother called to me, "Kit its yours."

The hare for a second was almost running towards me, I could see her eyes, there was something eerie about this hare, the eyes were not looking at me, they were on the side of her head, and she was coming straight at me. Suddenly the hare's head turned slightly, now I was able to focus on the creature's black pupil, and what a view I got. I looked into a window of thousands of years of persecution, of Druid worship and speeding bullets ending precious lives, times of the chase, bending and turn elusively to shake off determined pursuers. This was not an animal, it was a witch, a goddess, a will o the wisp and I was going to catch it.

Never had I run as fast to match such speed, a speed that altered my sight into tunnel vision, focussed on only one thing, oblivious to dangers that common sense always guided me to avoid. Rabbit speed that seemed to be too fast for me when I was younger was now my second gear, and I took them with contemptuous ease. But as I've already said, these are not rabbits. A new set of gears were needed to be sought, to find a swiftness that tested every part of my young body's design.

On the back of this athlete I ran, quickly my mind deciphered her complicated running code, and I began to anticipate when she was going to jink or turn. The hare began to call out, her screams throwing every epithet of damnation at me to try and put me off. We were now as one, locked like gladiators in mortal combat, defeat was not a cloak to wear on this wild and windy night, and to end the contest I threw myself headlong at the hare, clamping my jaws over her thick, well muscled back.

This creature that had been brought up by an affectionate mother as I had, but who had been adopted by a surrogate parent, Mother Nature, lay dying, gasping for air that was never going to come. She kicked a couple of times, stared into my soul then solemn stillness as her life's blood trickled onto the soft soil. The eyes that earlier had given such a vivid insight to her history had closed their shutters. Her last dream, my first hare.

Now I had tasted the sweet delights of hare, rabbits that had given me so much satisfaction in my early life now became boring. They were no longer a test, but how could I let my master know? I think my master must have been able to sense this, because when I couldn't be bothered to run rabbits, he always took me for a trip to catch a hare.

Hare were chased with my master's light to guide me, but also when it was daylight. Not sure which I preferred, I enjoyed both, and caught hares no matter if an owl was hooting in the background, or a sweet melody of a linnet swaying on a sprig of yellow flowered gorse.

Then came deer

Although I knew that rabbits were my master's favourite creatures to chase, his excitement could always be detected by my finely honed senses when my mother or I caught a hare. On my first encounter with a deer however, I witnessed a side of my master that had never manifested before. A mixture of excitement, fear and pleasure.

It was again a wild night when we hunted, my master for some reason always picked these hostile evenings to take us out, I'm sure he must be frightened by the moon, and uncomfortable with a still breathless night. This evening was a family affair, my mother Bes, my dad Paddy and me. My dad had never hunted with me as much as my mam, when I saw him running he never quite matched the speed of my mother. He was a determined runner, who would run through a brick wall if he had to. Mam said he hated cats, foxes and anything that bit back, and these creatures always made him very angry. He would never pick a fight with another dog, but he would never back down if a dog picked on him. Mother often told me of times when he ripped a scrap yard guard dog to pieces, and also when he threw a wicked bull terrier cross all over the allotments in Ashington. Dad could really take care of himself.

It was not as far to travel that night, to a place called Tranwell Wood. In fields of young corn we tread, searching amid the shadows with every swishing sweep of my master's light. Hares and rabbits flashed through my mind, until suddenly the beam of light detected two big blue eyes in the distance.

"Deer," my master's friend called out excitedly. Both my parents set off down the lamp's beam, I followed keeping up just behind my dad's black and tan backside. We ran until for the first time I saw what a deer actually was. It was massive, just as tall as me, it had a big white backside, and bloody horns on the top of its head. Surely it was a mistake. Surely we weren't expected to catch one of these.

Like hares and rabbits these deer ran quite fast, and even jinked like hares at times. My mother did all the work on this big hare, keeping it from getting into the woods. The deer turned and ran towards my dad, who smashed into it like a car raid on a bank cash machine. I got there and sank my teeth into it, but dad turned on me and bit me, I never got over this. My master, who by the way is the slowest runner I have ever seen, eventually got to the deer that now had both my parents on it. My master pulled my dad off, and told me to "get in". I obliged and bit hard at the creature's throat. Another new animal for me, and another beautiful taste and sensation. My master's friend carried the deer on his shoulders when it was dead; I jumped up at it when possible for another bite, keeping an eye on my dad, the old grumpy bastard, just in case he got a bit snappy at me again.

For seven years my life was with my master. My dad died after breaking his leg chasing a rabbit in Scotland, and even though it wasn't my master's dog, he cried over this and his sadness was there for all to see for many months. I never had any children of my own, but my master did get another pup, Yella who he got bred off my brother Cap. What a lovely puppy she was, and I played with her much of the time, she brought out the puppy in me. Yella had a specialness about her, and I loved every minute of her company.

For a time my master had to move our shed down to the allotments, I didn't enjoy this as much as living at home, I didn't see my master, my mistress or their pups as much now, but my master came to visit me and feed me every day, rain, hail or snow. We still hunted as much as we always did, and this helped with the agony of missing what I had been brought up with.

One night I heard the gate to the allotment open, excitement flooded through my body, and we all jumped up at the bars of the run looking forward to once again being out in the fields. I heard a loud noise, like metal being violently snapped. Two strangers entered my shed; these were humans I recognised by their smell, people who had passed our allotment many times in the past, and had even spoken to my master.

I was wary, I growled and bared my teeth as a torch was shone at me by these faceless humans, a neck squeezer was fitted around my neck and I was taken from my shed.

I never saw my master again, so this dear reader, is where my story must end.

CHAPTER 17

Old Yella

THE THREE best all-round hunting dogs that I have owned that could be categorized as being true "profit hunters' dogs" are Bes, Kit and Yella. Both Bes and Kit have already designated chapters, it is now the turn of another great dog that caught unimaginable amounts of quarry species for me, and for who I shed many tears when she passed away to that big coursing ground in the skies.

Yella came at a time of my hunting life when interests of taking bigger quarry or those creatures that bite back were beginning to wane. I was drifting back towards what had always been a much safer prey to take illicitly, rabbits. Even hare that had run with dogs for many decades, I was loosing interest in. Not that I ever thought that this bitch was incapable of achieving success against this mammalian athlete, far from it. Yella was bred from a line of dogs that at times could make taking hares look easy and their peers ordinary, but I wanted a rabbit dog, and that's what Yella was carefully moulded into.

My father instilled in me the chain of thought that man with his juggling could breed anything, except a bird with three eyes. I knew in my mind's eye what I wanted in running dogs that fitted my needs, and my father coached me into achieving this. My aim was to produce dogs that were intelligent, smallish, but not too fine that they could not withstand the rigours of excessive work on all quarry that I hunted. I wanted dogs that were fast but able to stick with even the tightest turning hare, dogs with incredible endurance with a hunting temperament that ensured they would never give in. Don't we all I can almost hear being screamed at these pages, but this is what we bred, a fact that can be backed up by anyone who travelled with me with any of these three lurchers. Small dogs begat from big dogs, breeding down, rather than using whippet blooded lurchers, and breeding up.

Another one of our plans was to try and breed parents that "clicked". We saw there was a buff and yellow in dogs as there are in bird breeding. The perfect breeding for us being a mating of a yellow to a buff, a smooth coated dog being the yellow, and a rough dog being classed as the buff. Breeding two yellows (smooth coated) together would directly assist in producing a majority of offspring that would be too fine, and breeding together two buffs (rough coated) would lead to a greater percentage of offspring that would be coarse of cloddy. Disagree if you wish, but this was our premises, this was our lurcher breeding plan.

Even in breeds where there are traditionally no smoothed animals, such as the Scottish deerhound, the experienced eye can single out

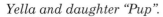

Yella and daughter "Pup".

animals that could be classed as yellows and buffs. Our Doxhope breed of deerhounds we saw as being predominantly yellows, finer boned animals, and breeding females that would always require bigger, coarse males to "click" with and produce deerhounds that matched the original standard of this most noble hound, and what "we" and many hundreds of people that contacted us after seeing and making comparisons with wolfhound look a likes were wishing to possess.

Yellow wasn't bred by us, but she was begat from our breeding. I looked towards progeny produced by a sibling from the same litter as Kit when this bitch was stolen by locals that believed they had more right to her than me. Kit's brother Cap, a smooth red lurcher had been mated to a rough haired bitch of good ability and I chose Yella at the ripe old age of five weeks, I obtained her at six weeks and from there this bitch became one of the legends of rabbit catching lurchers in mid to north Northumberland. She also produced progeny as good or in some ways better than her in certain departments, showing how pre-potent our breed had become, passing on the traits we saw as being "desirable".

Every lurcher that I've bred and kept for myself I have set a target of 100 rabbits before being a year old, Yella easily met this goal. From an early age we detected that this bitch was something special. Looking back, Yella being stolen would have been a much greater loss to our kennel than was the loss of my adored Kit.

During Yella's early career I witnessed this bitch taking numbers of rabbits during the hours of darkness that others could only dream of. Yes, the profit hunter worked lands that housed a veritable plethora of rabbits, but they still have to be caught, they certainly don't as some people believe, jump into your carrying bag. I've heard it all by novices over the years attempting to justify why they don't get such numbers when out hunting. "They are easy rabbits up there where you're going." "They give up." "You must have got a lot of squatters on the night."

Bunkem, pure bunkem, and like I say, "Novices".

Yella, like every dog, had her off nights. I witnessed her missing her first half a dozen rabbits on a night's lamping, but then I've also been privileged to other evenings when she caught 20 consecutive good running bunnies.

In the numbers' game, I have only witnessed one other dog that secured more nightly tallies of 30 plus, and that was Yella's daughter Sophie, co-produced by Billy Mercel's dog Blue, also a most proficient

The humble rabbit.

taker of large numbers of rabbits. But it wasn't only the then magical number of 30 rabbits in one night on these "easy" rabbits, Yella broke into 40s, 50s, 60s and 70s many times, and once into the 80 rabbits in one night. Could she have achieved the mystical 100 rabbits in one night, possibly on the ground that we hunted, on one of the rabbit infested Scottish Isle? Definitely. Why didn't she some may ask, but we have to remember this was poaching, starting our nightly vigil after 1am in the morning, and finishing at a time before conscientious farm hands and shepherds or keen keepers were up and about. On the night Yella caught 80 and her daughter Sophie took 81, both dogs could have taken more if our profit hunting discipline, an ethos that ensured we didn't want to get apprehended or fined hadn't kicked in. Yes, looking back I wish we had gone on to get the ton, but we did achieve a number that only a handful of dogs in the country have come anywhere close to.

Squatting rabbits. I once heard a lurcherman call this a "good fault". Statements akin to this never cease to amaze me. To the profit hunter, a dog that can do this can be a godsend, being able to hunt for much longer, with less stress and strain on muscles and tendons, conserving its energy for when it is needed, if the sights are switched to a hare or deer on the same night, or coursing hares in the daylight on the way home. Yella was never an aficionado of taking squatters, unlike her grandmother Bes who was a joy to watch, almost belly crawling at times up to rabbits lying still amid damp border grass, or shooting in from the side of the beam's glare out of the darkness picking up unsuspecting rabbits with contemptuous ease.

Yella's trait was more of pacing herself towards the squatting rabbit, as if wanting the creature to lift, sometimes standing motionless with me whispering "go on Yella, get in". She would then rush in with a burst of speed, usually picking up the rabbit after a few yards as the creature attempted to make its hasty escape.

During the 1990s I was a practicing mole man, clearing mole-infested Northumbrian landscapes ensuring the landowners silage never became a fermenting poisonous feed for their stock to consume. Whenever I set traps or placed strychnine covered earth worms into main and feeding runs, Yella always accompanied me and at times what interesting conversations we had. Like a statue she would sit watching as I did my part time work. She wasn't there as an observer however, and many times I watched her taking rabbits and hares and on one occasion she took 20 rabbits in one day off the fells around Elsdon as I controlled the moles.

Yella was almost a reincarnation of her grandmother Bes, 23.5 inches at the shoulder and weighing around 45lbs when fit. Yella as with her grandmother and her aunty Kit was extremely tight when chasing. Yella possessed more of Bes's hunting temperament than that of Kit's, and she just couldn't be sickened. As I've already stated, Kit did require the occasional bigger quarry to rejuvenate her rabbit hunting desire, a facet that both Bes and Yella didn't demand.

People often state their opinions of the easiness of a dog in taking rabbits on the lamp. In some situations and with the right dog this can be so, but over the years I've seen more dogs collapse when lamping rabbits than I have dogs folding up when coursing hares in daylight or ferreting during the day. So lamping can be a quite demanding pastime.

Catching rabbits in the daytime with dogs while combined with bolting them with ferrets is a hobby that I truly consider as "easy". Just as easy as I see killing hares at corn cuttings. I remember times when Yella worked with ferrets, and instances when she took over 40 rabbits in one day. Easy or not, as a profit hunter I may require methods that are possibly going to ensure more rabbits than means where we are only going to get a small number of bunnies. If I had an order of 40 rabbits I would certainly not go for daylight mooch.

Yella on hares. As I've already stated, with Yella my aim was to have an incredible rabbiting dog, a profit hunter's tool and in her 13 years on this earth she caught less than 20 hares and I can calculate on one hand how many roe deer she accounted for.

It was a wild windy night when Yella in her twelfth year told me she wanted to call it a day, not by voice, but by performance. This little friend wanted to do what she had always done, but her body on this night showed signs that it could not match what I demanded.

Then a year into retirement and a small blue lump appeared on one of her nipples, and grew to the size of a golf ball. Then one day when I entered her kennel, her lustrous eyes looked up at me, sad, almost telling me what I didn't want to hear. Yella had chewed into the cancerous swelling that I had been monitoring, and had left a hole in her side that I could almost put my hand into. Her time was up and I tearfully carried her all the way to the vet's in my arms, her warm body wrapped in a tartan car blanket, tears from my eyes rolling down my face.

I knelt on the floor, her black head resting on my thigh, I was sobbing like a child until the first injection took effect. The second injection came, then to peaceful sleep for my beloved Yella. A kiss on the top of her head as my tears fell amid her ebony fur was my last physical contact to send her on her way.

Old Yella was the last dog that I ever shed a tear for when they passed away. Never did I make such an attachment again. Yella was a lurcher but she was much more that just a dog, a tool of the trade, she was a faithful friend from whom I obtained so much joy and satisfaction. A profit hunter's dog.

CHAPTER 18

A Close Shave

MY INVOLVEMENT in the countryside has spanned well over five decades, and in that time, yes, there have been many changes. In its most unproductive form change can be terrifying, change can summon up so many demons that drive people into sheer panic and irrational thinking, but change also has a positive side to it, even if at first any amendment to what is the "norm" may take on a more negative guise. We profit hunters are a diverse breed, and the need to adapt is part of our genetic makeup, a survival strategy. Lesser mortals have come onto the hunting scene akin to lions, and in a short period of time have left like lambs at the first sign of that terrifying fiend, change.

The focus in this chapter highlights what was to be an advance for the boys in blue who had the sometimes frustrating task of trying to apprehend the profit hunters, after a late telephone call from an irate landowner or fuming gamekeeper. I wrote many years ago a premise that the greatest threat to illicit nocturnal hunting activities was communication. We hunt like shadows while the countryside sleeps, we have darkness, the greatest cloaking device to shroud our activities and we hide behind trees, so it will take a good man or poor misjudgement to catch us. In the 1990s however, another weapon was added to the police arsenal in an attempt to apprehend that most dangerous criminal the poacher, and this was the helicopter.

It was a cold November evening when my hunting partner and I left the warmth of our homes and travelled the relatively short distance to fields running alongside the A19 that always housed an abundance of partridges, an area close to the Tyne tunnel.

We parked the Daihatsu Fourtrak in a housing estate in the village of West Allotment, blending in with other cars and vans already settled down for the evening. We walked unassumingly through the estate, my friend carrying the lamping equipment, and me with the trusty 4.10 folded up and hidden in the confines of my well worn and battery acid eaten Barbour jacket. At the edge of the estate we entered the fields through a well trodden gap in a most untidy hedgerow, hawthorn and blackthorn bushes littered with flapping paper, cardboard boxes and sheets of polythene. In the shadows of the field we waited a short time, allowing the land to settle, and to observe our doorway to the setting, ensuring there were no nosey parkers following us, and nobody likes a nosey parker.

A couple of two and a half inch magnum cartridges were inserted into the little gun's chambers, and we were on our way, the beam of light from our lamp scanning the land for our prey.

It didn't take long before a covey of partridges was spotted at the edge of the beam, a dark shadow-like group squatting on the finely tilled soil. No reflection of eyes acting as a giveaway to their location, just our experience of past partridge hunting adventures that guided us towards the tightly packed half sleeping cluster. Slowly we approached, drifting across the land cat-like, silently, stealthily with the light remaining on all the time, as experience had taught us the light being switched off and trying to walk in the dark towards partridges will only spook the birds, they will lift and the hunting opportunity will be lost.

Closer and closer we moved till the distance was right for this gun to have maximum effect. The hunters paused, breath was held momentarily and two hearts beat so fast and loud they almost spooked the resting covey. The barrels of the gun smoothly rose pointing directly towards the centre of the group of birds, both triggers pulled in unison releasing an angry blast, followed by explosion of deathly silence. The deed was done.

Now came a time of excited commotion, and the spoils were collected, birds in their last throws of life littering the small epicentre, the lamp needing to be switched on at intervals as a pricked bird bounced and bounded across the ground until caught. When all the birds were collected, they were lain on the ground and once again, a time of rest for the land and a moment to focus on our surroundings to ensure that

The police helicopter.

the hunter was not about to become the hunted. We had secured quite a good return of 11 birds for our first shot of the evening.

To folk who have never participated in this form of poaching it may sound like the catalyst for disaster, shining a light in a field at 8 o'clock at night, then firing a noisy scatter gun, but these assumptions are only partly correct. People sitting in their cosy living rooms watching their favourite soaps even a relatively short distance from the fields will never hear the bang from this type of gun. Discharging the weapon will sound loud to the person pulling the trigger or his accomplice standing close to hand, but at a distance this bang will become a muffled thud, undetectable to most people. Even in these semi urban areas the profit hunter will have to be unlucky to be detected by someone who is more au fait with guns, lamping and poaching and who is passing the area at just the wrong time. Little did we know at this point, just that type of person had passed and had notified the feds.

After a short time and with confidence restored we lifted the assembled birds and placed them in our carrying bag, the gun was once again loaded, and we set off into the darkness, scanning for more birds. Zigzagging the field we searched and our endeavours were rewarded by the taking of three more partridge coveys. Then our first alert to something being not quite right.

Knowing the lie of the land we were aware of not only the main A19 dual carriageway but also a couple of smaller roads that at times bordered onto the fields we were working. It was on one of these roads where we saw the flash of blue lights, lights that only stayed on for a few seconds, then went off. We now sat in total darkness, watching, assessing, with a little apprehension now creeping into our proceedings.

"Well it was definitely a police car," I said calmly to my chum.

We planned to sit it out for a while, no policeman will leave the warmth of his "panda car" to tread across muddy fields looking for people who most probably would be away by now. They would be sitting watching, for a light that was never going to go on again and we sat waiting to hear the engine of their car droning into the distance before we made another move. A war of silent attrition ensued.

Minutes later high above our heads in the distance the drone of a helicopter could be heard, unperturbed at this point, we even discussed with each other that it could possibly be the new police helicopter that had been documented recently in the local newspapers and on local TV news programmes. Closer and closer the helicopter came, louder and louder the noise of its engine could be heard, not the slow pounding drone of a two-bladed Chinook, but definitely resonating noise that almost matched the simple harmonic motion of our heartbeats.

Again the blue lights towards the road flashed, this time however followed by the intense beam of light emanating from the helicopter above us, it was becoming one of those situations where the hunter was definitely going to become the prey.

It was now time for action, our equipment was quickly gathered and we ran away from the hot spot of the light, which was focussing almost in the centre of the field. We were however, running towards the entrance to our field, a way in yes, but not an exit, we paused, questioning each other for a plan.

"We will make for the dual carriageway," I said, the words almost unable to come from my burning throat. They will never shine that light on the main road for the cars was my thinking.

166

It's amazing how far the sanctuary we seek becomes when you are being pursued. It took what seemed like a lifetime to reach a fence tangled with dense, clothes-grabbing brambles, with the light that sought us closely following. In unison we dived almost headlong into the prickly fortress, and like rabbits we weaved our way through the undergrowth with a total disregard to prickly claw-like thorns. We made our way up the embankment towards the road, and my assumption was correct, the helicopter made its way searchingly back into the field, taking the white light with it.

As luck would have it, we emerged on the road a few yards away from a parking place, here we hid our gun, lamp and battery and bags of lifeless birds behind the only bush on the lay-by, all the time keeping close watch on the helicopter frantically searching for us.

Again we waited, watching and assessing the situation. We decided to walk along the A19 northwards back towards the village, nipping into the bushes or hiding in the long grass on the road verge every time car headlights approached. Eventually we came to a place where a path made its way down the embankment. The helicopter was now in the distance and posed us no imminent threat, so we headed down the slippery, sloping trail.

We came to the estate where our vehicle was parked, but a police car stood sentinel at the entrance to the street, and the commotion had encouraged a group of spectators who gazed into the sky akin to a Spielberg film. We avoided entering the street as an old woman passed.

"Whats going on darling?"

"It's the police helicopter after someone son," she replied in a friendly Mrs Know All type of voice.

"You just never know who's knocking about these days hinny," I facetiously replied, and we moved on.

At the other end of the village there was a pub, and we entered looking for a telephone to call for assistance. It was pointless waiting to get the jeep, so we phoned my dad to come and get us. We searched our pockets and between us we had enough for a couple of glasses of coke, as we are both teetotal. Within half an hour my dad arrived, and we left for home, and safety, giving my dad all the grisly details on the way back.

The next day I was at work and during the morning I tested a bus after a repair, stopping in the lay-by and picking up all our gear. After work my dad took me over to West Allotment to collect my car.

This night was to be a test to our bush craft and stealth in the face of adversity, and an insight to the future. Had that early helicopter been equipped with the heat seeking cameras that later helicopter have, we would have no doubt been apprehended, dragged out of the undergrowth like rabbits being pulled from their holes by a keen ferreter.

We did escape and two nights later we were out again, in a different location of course, not wanting to have another "close shave".

CHAPTER 19

The Court Jesters

THERE COMES a time in every profit hunter's life when a mistake will be costly. Blunders that if it had occurred in the olden days would have cost an eye, a hand or a long journey to a hostile foreign land. Through skill and guile I can brag that in over 40 years I have been to court once and fined twice and when considering how many tons of rabbits, thousands of game birds and hundreds of hares, deer and kings of the sea I have been party to taking, well I think I have come through it pretty well intact.

My first error happened across the borders when a group of us were spotted ferreting in a field by a farmer doing an early morning check of his stock. Seeing the old truck cab Landrover chugging past and hearing the challenging blare of its horn and a wrinkled fist shaking out of the driver's side window, well we should have guessed he wasn't inviting us to the next young farmer's ball.

A ferret holed up ensured we took more time in getting away from an environment that assumed a more inhospitable feel about it by the minute. Then, as if half expected, a police car pulled up and the old Landrover close behind.

The two policemen climbed the drystone wall and approached.

"Hello boys, what you up to?"

"A spot of ferreting," I replied.

"Have you got permission?" Well I could hardly say yes with the Jock farm hand sitting watching from the sanctuary of his four-wheel drive. Plead ignorant Bill, it's your only chance I thought to myself.

"No, we are only after a few rabbits, and our ferret is stuck down the hole."

Then came the customary telling us we were trespassing in pursuit of game, followed by writing of names and reading of rights. We were well and truly done.

When everything was sorted, I asked the policemen if we could get the ferret, and they watched till we were sorted and off the land. We were then escorted through Grantshouses, down the A1 to Berwick. A few months later after pleading guilty by letter, our names were in the Journal, and a penalty of £50 was imposed by Sheriff Patterson at Dun's sheriffs' court.

Over 20 years later, and again over the border another slip-up, this time it was more costly, a £150 fine (paid off at £2 per week) and the confiscation of a good air rifle.

We had been lamping fields that sloped up toward the Lammermuir Hills, near the Whiteadder reservoir all night, two of us, three dogs and we had secured a quite impressive haul of 93 rabbits. We lay half asleep in a lay-by on the moors, cat napping waiting for daylight to break bringing with it the haunting cries of patrolling curlews that circled high above us. It was time, the slowly brightening skies signalling for us to move on in search of blue hares.

There is a single road that runs across the Lammermuirs, from Longframacus to Gifford, snaking across terrains that rise and fall, following the rugged contours of these ancient lands. Driving slowly along this track, keen eyes watch for movement amid the heather. If a hare is spotted, doors are quickly opened and our dogs are released and the spectacle is watched from the roadside, no need to trespass, if the hare is caught the dogs will bring it back to the waiting hands of their masters.

We travelled as always along this road, and secured five hares that morning. On reaching the outskirts of Longframacus village, we usually call it a day and head for home. This morning, we decided to go back over the same road, and go home via a different route, through Cranshaws, where it is facetiously said that people living there eat their young.

Again we coursed hares, but this time, with a Sharps pump up air rifle we also decided to take some of the land's overstocking of red grouse. When shooting game birds from the car like this, no feathers should be left as tell tail signs for any prying eyes to find. Birds are put straight into plastic carriers, outside the car. That morning we shot eight birds, four birds in two bags were hidden under the front seats of our car.

High on the hills we came to a junction and turned right for home. We had just got round the corner when a car approached, a police car.

Time to panic

The loaded gun was discharged out of the window and shoved down the side of the passenger seat. The dogs were ordered to lie down as the car passed, the occupants staring intensely at us, we trying not to make eye contact and acting as innocent holidaymakers.

In the mirror I saw the red brake lights go on, then the car maneuvering on the narrow road, doing what resembled a 50-point turn. On reflection, our first failing was going back over the moors for a second run, error two was shooting grouse, and mistake three was not throwing the bags of birds out the window when we had the opportunity.

We were followed and pulled over. Questions were asked, and at one point it did seem as if we had made it, even though our haul of rabbits with the hares hidden beneath had been seen. However, the hawk like eyes of the younger policeman spotted the bags under the seats.

"What's in them bags?" he asked.

"What bags?"

"Those bags under the seat," he said angrily. Without another word I pulled the bags from their hiding place and passed them to the policeman's waiting hand. That was that, everybody out. Our spoils were taken, as was the rifle, lamps and batteries. Had we only had rabbits, we would definitely have been ok, game birds well that's a different ball game. Another court visit imminent.

Over the weeks we decided that we were going to plead guilty by letter, until we read the summons from Haddington sheriff's court, which stated possible maximum fine of up to £1,000 and/or six months in jail.

"Audrey, Audrey get me the number of a good Jock solicitor."

Our date with the sheriff was eventually set, and because of it being a long journey to Haddington, we decided to take the dogs and go lamping first, hide the lamps and any spoils we obtained on the night then go straight to the court for 10am. We took only two dogs that evening before our court appearance, and caught over 70 rabbits, to sell towards the petrol costs and fines.

In the morning as planned, we hid the rabbits before going on to Haddington and finding the court. We parked our car up in the car park and went to sleep for an hour. My slumber was annoyingly disturbed by a knock on the car window. At first I thought I was dreaming, a black monk was standing next to me, peering at me with devilish eyes.

"Are you Mr Doherty," he asked.

"Aye," I replied, rubbing my eyes and wiping the saliva dribbling from my mouth. This man was our solicitor.

"Quickly, we are late, we have to get into the court."

"No time to freshen up and powder our noses then," I murmured.

With litigation and some good work by our solicitor, some of the charges were dropped, we were prosecuted under section 1 of the Firearms Act, as they had tested the air rifle and said it was producing over 20 pounds feet, well over the legal limit of 12. Brazing that valve certainly did the trick. We were also done for the grouse and the hares, but not the rabbits, we got our lamps and batteries back but not the gun and we were told that the rabbits originally held as evidence had been spoilt.

After thanking the solicitor with a good firm handshake we left, and just as we pulled away there was such a grinding on the front end of the car.

"What the hell now," I blurted out.

The pads were that far down it was now metal to metal on the discs. No garage, no money so we drove from Haddington over the Lammermuirs to pick up the rabbits and back to Ashington with no brakes as such.

That was the last time I was caught for poaching, yes some near misses over the years, but many lessons that were learnt by these episodes stuck with me, and helped ensure that no Scottish sheriff or English magistrate would ever look over their square gold rimmed glasses at me again.

CHAPTER 20

Today's
Profit Hunters

EVEN THOUGH part of me still resides in a time where rush and push were not allowed, a secret place, where the negative thoughts that tend to accompany adulthood are forbidden, I remain a pure bred profit hunter. I still believe Mother Nature is a hot chick and Jack Frost is a cool guy and I will always be found guilty of that hideous crime of consuming more than my allotted share of pleasure from the countryside of Great Britain.

A date or time cannot be given when my move away from killing the creatures that in many ways I envied took place. Maybe it was the same time when my raven black hair took on shall we say a much lighter but distinguished colouration. Or possibly the same time when wrinkles slyly took residence on my face or when a big chunk of my family passed away taking with it a massive piece of my soul. Sad times, but Mother Nature has the knack of putting the brightness back into otherwise miserable eyes.

Having been blessed with a memory that has the ability to retain almost photographic evidence of what transpired so many decades ago, and an imagination with the talent of fashioning so many wonderful creations to keep my body occupied, these and other genetic traits would never allow me to think of not being a hunter. But with age came a mellowing process. Desires are quenched, tempers lengthen due to a form of male menopause ensuring that one becomes a completely different person. A new persona that can be quite difficult to come to terms with at times.

The author as a mole man.

Nowadays the drive to take game has almost been laid to rest. No longer do I possess the desire to kill. Deer, fox or a hare and even rabbits are now safe from this ageing profit hunter. However, I am far from being a broken man. This fresh person still possesses the same affinity with wildlife, which has moved in a different direction, but I remain a profit hunter.

Today sees me shooting with a camera, getting into positions where I steal images not lives, witnessing the wondrous beauty of creatures

The Bee Eater.

I pursue but leaving them in their natural settings for others to enjoy.

The catalyst for change, apart from age and all the signs associated with it probably spiralled with the death of my father, a man I worshipped like a god, and with whom I still have associations and conversations when eyelids are tightly closed. When he departed from this earth he took with him many things from me, including my desire to hunt, as if telling me enough was enough. My dad was extremely proud of what I did in my hunting capacity, and would brag about my achievements to all and sundry, and why not, he was my main mentor. Everything I did or attempted to achieve in my lifetime was for him.

What my dad left as his legacy for me was this affinity with wildlife that he instilled in me at conception, unscathed, a commanding driving force that pushes me when feelings of foreboding enter into my life, and how proud he would be on seeing my photographs and reading my books or witnessing my work with the younger generation who seem to automatically want to be involved with our British fauna and flora.

My life is now taking steps downwards on the staircase towards my final resting place, but this cannot halt my hunting

The Kingfisher.

The Osprey - one of our most dramatic profit hunters.

for profit, however. Times have dramatically changed, and I have mentioned how my main weapon is my camera, and the tools of my trade are no longer gaffs, longnets or fit lurcher dogs. These have been replaced with telephoto lenses, a ghullie suit and a pop-up hide. The bush craft so cleverly added into my life by skilled mentors who knew so many diverse country crafts is still put to excellent use. The ghosts of some of these masters will proudly watch through the mists of time as I stealthily move into positions where I can photograph bird and beast in their natural setting, this is where I now obtain so much satisfaction, and profit.

As a wildlife photographer I am not, and could never afford to go on monthly jaunts to far off places in search of that outstanding image of creatures that only a handful of homosapiens will have the privilege of being intimate with. I am more of an opportunist wildlife photographer, focussing on the flora and fauna endemic to my native Northumberland, with occasional saved up for jaunts over the Scottish borders. Why travel to exotic places, when all I desire is practically on my door step? Northumberland and the borders of ancient Caledonia.

Scotland for me is a magical place; it feels so much different to any other location. Never do I tire on crossing the border at Carter Bar and heading towards towering hills scattered with powdery lavender, the strident call of red grouse telling intruders to "go, back, back, back".

The author, wildlife photographer.

Red squirrels.

A male sparrowhawk.

Over 30 years ago these jaunts would have involved taking a longnet or a pair of keen hunting dogs.

I consider myself to be so fortunate in what I have seen and done in a hunting capacity, the likes of which not many men will ever again be party to, but I also feel privileged to what I have observed and captured through the eye piece of a good quality camera.

This final chapter of revelations of my hunting life may seem to some younger hunters of today as a coward's way out, an opt out clause for an old gunslinger silently waiting for the up and coming to take over. But being at the top never lasts forever, we move on to what is acceptable and more importantly, achievable.

To show how I have adapted, and how I now survive I have included some of my favourite images of wildlife friendships from planned and unplanned photographic jaunts. I hope you dear reader have enjoyed viewing these as we part company.

Before the door is temporarily closed, I hope you have benefited from what has been written, and to understand what my aim was with the creation of this countryside book, and what I wanted to come across to you on every page, every chapter, every sentence and every word.

An aim that was to show in many diverse ways we are all "Profit Hunters".